SEASONS

A CURATED SELECTION OF TIMELY TECHNIQUES FROM THE PAGES OF FLORISTS' REVIEW

florists' review

"*The seasons are what a symphony ought to be: four perfect movements in harmony with each other.*"

Arthur Rubinstein, musician

In every season, flowers bring beauty and opportunity for creative expression. At *Florists' Review*, one of our goals is to support that spark of creativity, which is why, each month, we share detailed techniques and florist tips on how to design a variety of floral masterpieces.

We are thrilled to present this curated selection of the very best of our most popular and interesting "Technique" articles from the last two years. With deft hands and acute visual skill sets, these talented designers, photographers and writers continually transform blossoms, twigs and foliage with stunning success.

We give special thanks to those contributors, and our sponsors, for sharing their magic and showing us how to make all the seasons a blooming delight. Enjoy!

Travis

Travis Rigby, Publisher
Florists' Review

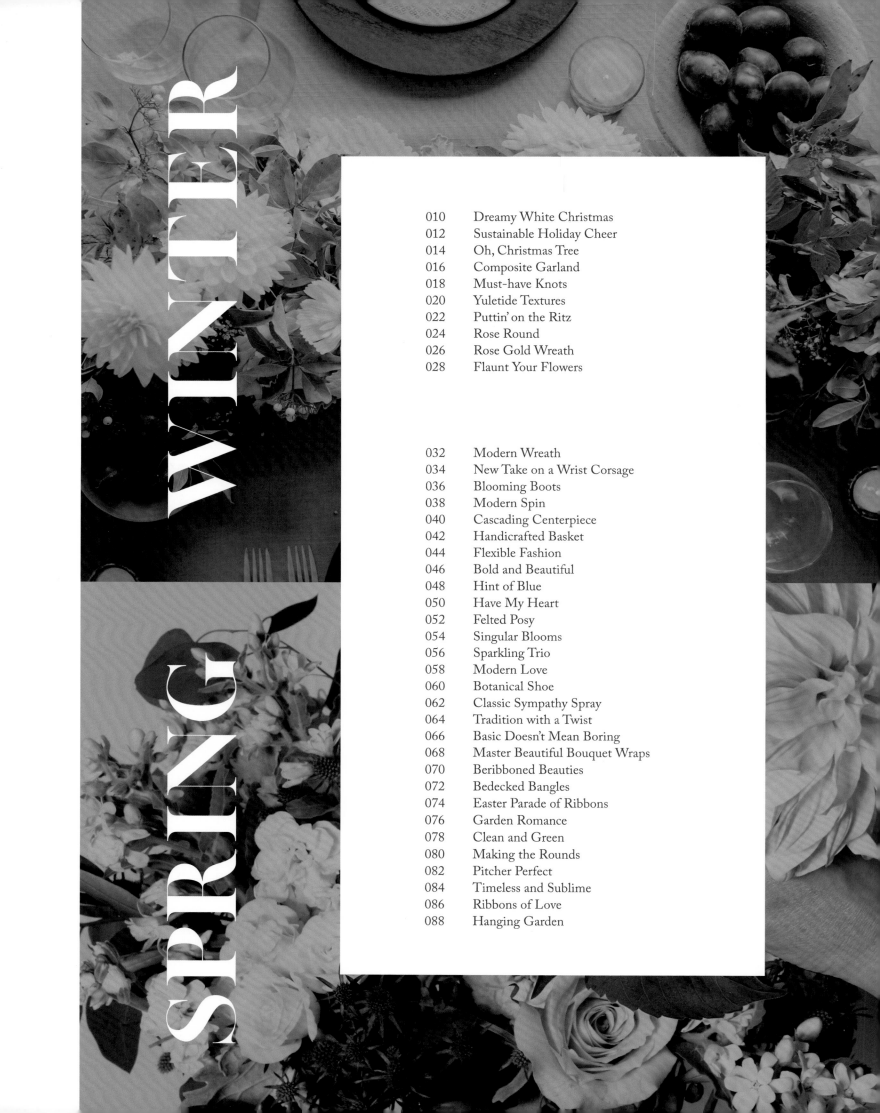

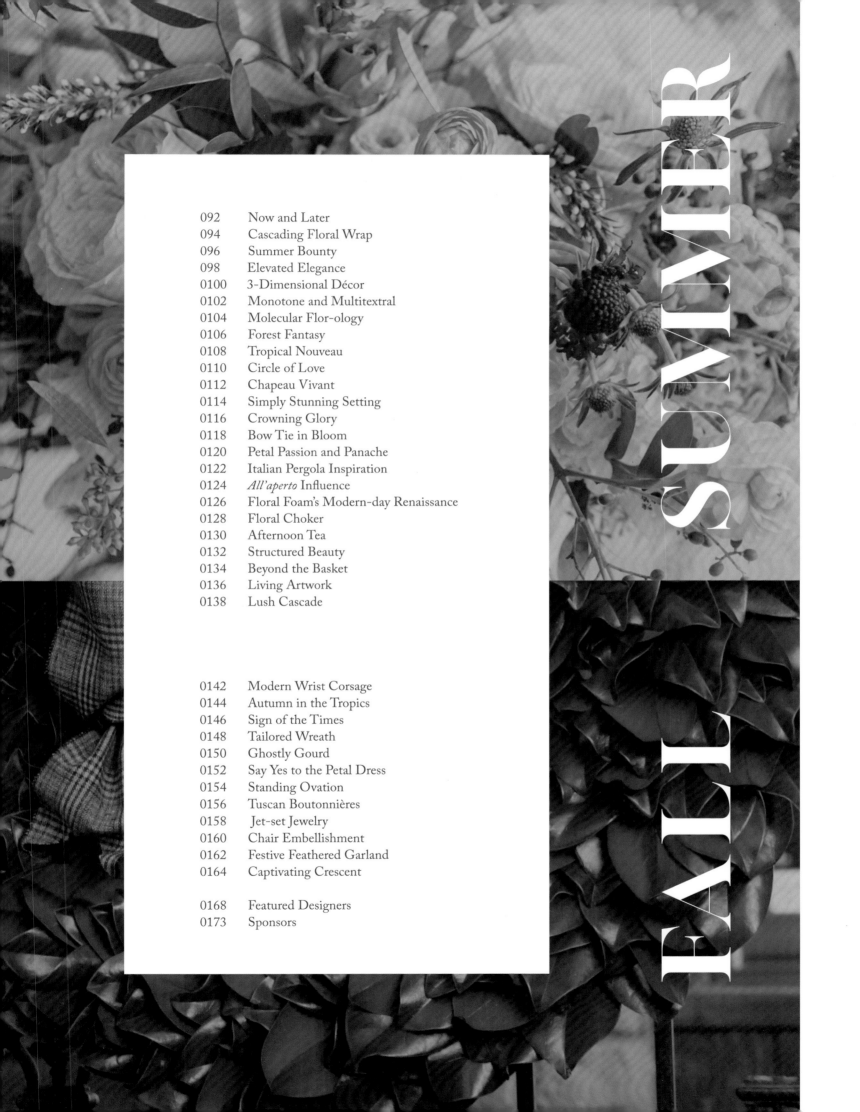

Photo by Amanda Dumouchelle Photography. See how-to design and steps on Pages 16-17.

WINTER

Hydrate stem sponge wraps in flower-food solution. **01**

Secure paddle wire to the wreath frame to get started, looping it over a joint in the frame. **05**

Gather flowers by variety, and trim the stems so the flower heads are staggered. **02**

Secure flower bundles to the wreath frame with paddle wire. Wire the bundles at the point bound with the rubber bands to further ensure no water leakage. **06**

Fold stem sponge wraps over the cut stems, and roll the wrap around each bundle of stems securely. **03**

Add a bit of painted fern between each bundle to help conceal the mechanics. **0**

Slide a plastic bag over each wrapped stem bundle, and secure with rubber bands. **04**

Work your way around the wreath frame, alternating flower type and adding sprigs of painted fern throughout. **0**

dreamy white
christmas

MATERIALS

Standard *Gerbera* "Pole Ice", Gerpom (cushion *Gerbera*) "Amando," white *Lisianthus/Eustoma grandiflora*, white snapdragon (*Antirrhinum majus*), white stock (*Matthiola incana*) and leatherleaf fern (*Rumohra* spp.) from **Rosa Flora**; Floral Hydration Stem Sponge-Wrap from **Eco Fresh Bouquet**; übermatte Color Finish (Crema) from **Design Master Color Tool**; 18" Wire Wreath Form from **FloraCraft**; Paddle Wire from **Syndicate Sales**.

Floral design by Susan McLeary • Photos by Amanda Dumouchelle

Place several potted cacti (seven in this design) randomly into the rectangular concrete container, and fill the container with gravel. **01**

Wrap several small plastic-foam wreath forms and orbs with yarns of your choice. Arrange them atop the planter, and secure them in place with wood picks, stakes or skewers. **02**

Insert the *Dahlia* stems into water tubes, and arrange them throughout the design. **03**

Add iridescent ornaments in random placements. **04**

Arrange small stems of *Brunia*, *Artemisia*, dried *Eryngium* and skeletonized leaves throughout the design. **05**

sustainable
holiday cheer

MATERIALS
Various potted cacti, ball-form *Dahlias*, *Brunia*, *Artemisia lactiflora* (white mugwort), dried *Eryngium* x *tripartitum* (sea holly), skeletonized leaves, rectangular concrete planter, yarn, gravel, wood picks, plastic-foam wreath forms and orbs, water tubes, iridescent ball ornaments.

Floral design by Arthur Williams, AIFD, EMC, CPF • Photos by Amanda Baker Photography

Spray paint a wood board, round or rectangular, with bronze paint. **01**

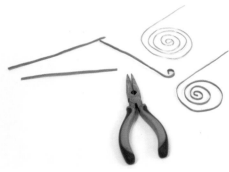

Using the jewelry pliers, create different sized spirals with aluminum wire and flat wire. **02**

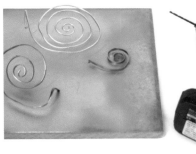

Drill small holes into the board, and glue the spirals into the holes, placing the spirals to create the shape of a Christmas tree. **03**

Cut pieces of red electrical wire, and interweave it between the spirals to complete the shape of the tree. **04**

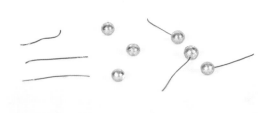

Cut small pieces of metallic wire, and glue mini spheres onto these wires. **05**

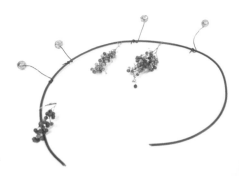

Wrap the metallic wire around the electrical wire to attach the spheres, and wire the pepperberry branches to the armature with bullion wire. **06**

Screw through the back of the board to attach the wood slices vertically to create the trunk of the Christmas tree. **07**

Form a star with baling wire, and wrap the star shape in bullion wire to create the tree topper. **08**

Wire water tubes with baling wire, and wrap the wire with floral tape. Spray paint the water tubes and wire with bronze paint to match the background. **09**

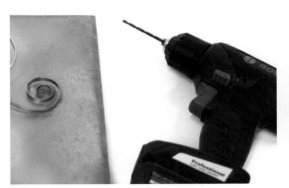

Drill new holes in the background board to glue the water tube wires into. **10**

Wind the flowers into the armature, using as much of the stem lengths as possible to create a lush and natural look. **11**

oh, christmas tree

MATERIALS

Phalaenopsis (moth) orchids; Strawflowers *(Helichrysum bracteatum / Xerochrysum)*; *Dahlia*; *Eustoma / Lisianthus*; Pepperberry *(Schinus molle)*; Switch grass *(Panicum virgatum)*; Board; Wood slices; Oasis Aluminum Wire (Gold, Brown); Oasis Flat Wire (Bronze); Oasis Metallic Wire (Brown); Oasis Bullion Wire (Gold), and Floratape Stem Wrap from **Smithers-Oasis North America**; Glittered mini spheres (Gold); Electrical wire (Red); Baling wire; Water tubes; Spray paint (Bronze); Liquid silicon adhesive; Drill; Jewelry pliers.

Floral design by Leopoldo Gomez • Photos by Bogar Marin

MATERIALS

'White Onesta' *Dahlia*; 'Sonata White' *Cosmos*; 'Quicksand' hybrid-tea roses; 'Rosanne Brown' *Lisianthus*; Red raspberry stems *(Rubus idaeus)*; Coral bells *(Huechera* spp.); 'New Look' dusty miller *(Senecio cineraria)*; Panicled dogwood *(Cornus racemosa)*; Autumn olive and Russian olive *(Elaeagnus* spp.); Prune plums *(Prunus* spp.); 3-inch Lomey Pedestal Foam and Oasis Bind Wire from **Smithers-Oasis North America**.

Layer the greenery and branches into attractive bundles, trim stems and secure with paper-covered wire. Eight to 10 bundles work well for an 8-foot-long table. The bundles can be made ahead of time and stored upright in buckets to continue to hydrate. Try other long-lasting greenery that will hold its shape, such as *Eucalyptus*, *Acacia* or olive branches *(Elaeagnus)*. **01**

Arrange the flowers and foliages into floral-foam cages — or other low containers — in a natural garden style, taking care to drape the ingredients over the edges to conceal the cages/containers. **02**

Line foliage bundles and garden "pods" along the center of the table, spacing the florals evenly. Place the foliage bundles facing the same direction so the ends of each can be tucked into the next placement and hidden. Turn the last bundle in the opposite direction, and tuck the stem ends into the body of the design. **03**

Add low bowls of fruit, candlesticks and votives to accent the design and add drama. **04**

composite garland

Floral design by Susan McLeary and Kirbey Rogic • Photos by Amanda Dumouchelle Photography

Fully hydrate a floral-foam wreath base, and then securely wrap heavy-duty plastic wrap (or waterproof ribbon) around the section of the wreath where ribbons will be tied. This keeps the ribbon from absorbing water from the wreath base. **01**

Spray the plastic-wrap-wrapped portion of the wreath with gold paint, and allow to dry. **02**

Cut lengths of ribbons long enough to wrap around the wreath, and then tie each one in a singular knot, side by side, around the plastic-wrap-wrapped section of the wreath. Create any pattern of repetition of your choice — even haphazard. **03**

Arrange sprigs of white pine around the inner and outer edges of the wreath base. **04**

Arrange the *Hydrangeas*, roses, *Astilbe*, *Brunia*, *Viburnum* berries and succulents into the wreath base. **05**

must-have knots

MATERIALS
Filigree Rococo Elegance Wired Edge (Ivory/Gold), Gold Bar Metallic Linen Wired Edge (White/Gold), Dupioni Tapestry Wired Edge (Antique Gold) and Dupioni Supreme Wired Edge (Ivory) from **Reliant Ribbons Bows & Trims**; *Rosa* 'Quicksand' (hybrid tea rose) from **Rio Roses**; Antique *Hydrangea*, *Astilbe* spp. (false spiraea), *Brunia albiflora*, *Viburnum* spp. berry, *Pinus strobus* (white pine) and 4" succulents from suppliers of your choice; 21" Oasis Wreath Base from **Smithers-Oasis North America**; Brilliant Gold Colortool Metals from **Design Master Color Tool**, glass ornaments from **Winward International/Jim Marvin Collection**, heavy-duty plastic wrap or waterproof ribbon.

Floral design and photos by Lori McNorton

Cut or tear pieces of handmade Japanese handmade paper (or similar texturized paper of choice) to desired size and width, enough to cover all sides of the container(s) as well as the wood elevation board.

01

Paint the board white, if you choose, and glue container(s) to a 2" x 4" board (length of your choice). Apply hot glue lightly to one long edge of a piece of paper, and press the paper vertically against the side of the container(s) and board. Continue this process until all sides of the container(s) and board are covered.

02

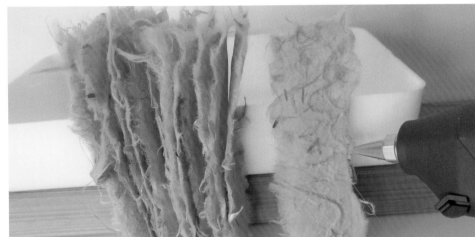

Place saturated floral foam into the container(s), and evenly distribute sand over the foam, just enough to cover the surface. Do not fill container(s) to the rim with sand.

03

Arrange stems of fresh and dried botanicals low to the surface of the sand-covered floral foam and within the paper borders, in a manner similar to that shown here. Lay air plants into the design to finish the composition.

04

yuletide textures

MATERIALS

Miniature callas (*Zantedeschia* spp.), miniature *Cymbidium* orchids and ball-form *Dahlias* from **FTD Flower Exchange**; dried bishop's weed/Queen Anne's lace (*Ammi majus*) and air plants (*Tillandsia*) from suppliers of your choice; Full-brick Trays (White) from **Diamond Line Containers**; sand from **Sandtastik Products**; Oasis Floral Foam Maxlife and Oasis All-temp Glue Sticks from **Smithers-Oasis North America**; handmade Japanese paper from craft store; 2" x 4" lumber from home-improvement store.

Floral design by Katharina Stuart, AIFD, CCF

MATERIALS

'Leona' Roselily (*Lilium* spp.) from **The Sun Valley Group**; spray roses (*Rosa* spp.) from **Green Valley Floral**; tuberoses (*Polianthes tuberosa*); White Shimmer plumosa from **FernTrust**; ostrich feathers from **Zucker Feather Products**; silver Jewel Ice and black Dupioni Supreme ribbons from **Reliant Ribbons Bows & Trims**; Super Nova CB Pin Dazzle from **Lion Ribbon Company**; Patrician Taper Candles from **Candle Artisans**; Mirror Strips Club Vase from **Jamali Floral & Garden Supplies**; Oasis Diamante Round Brooch, Oasis Floral Foam Maxlife and Oasis UGlu Adhesive Dashes from **Smithers-Oasis North America**; übermatte (Ink) from **Design Master Color Tool**; candlesticks and top hat from party store.

Assemble materials, and wrap bejeweled ribbon around the hat, securing the ends with adhesive strips. **01**

Wrap black silk ribbon around the mirrored container, and secure the ends with adhesive dashes. Attach the brooch to the container with an adhesive dash also. **02**

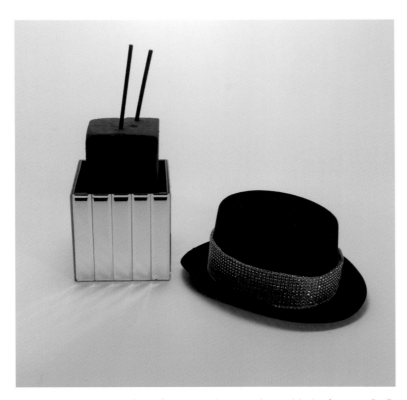

Insert floral foam into the container, with the foam extending out of the container about half the height of the container. Insert two wood dowels into the foam. **03**

Place the bedecked hat atop the dowels once the flowers and foliages are arranged into the floral foam. **04**

puttin' on the ritz

Floral design and photos by Lori McNorton

MATERIALS

'Mirabel' spray roses (*Rosa* spp.) from **California Pajarosa Floral**; 'Excellence' *Gypsophila* (baby's breath) from **Florabundance**; Charmelia spray *Alstroemeria* from **Gardens America**; *Eucalyptus sepulcralis* (blue weeping gum) from **Resendiz Brothers Protea Growers**; *Magnolia*; Christmas ball pick from **Hill's Imports/Park's Company**; red velvet ribbon from **Lion Ribbon Company**; ECOssentials Cylinders (Moss) and Oasis Clear Tape from **Smithers-Oasis North America**.

Create a checkerboard-like grid atop the container with clear waterproof tape. This grid is the armature that will hold the foliages and flowers. **01**

Arrange stems of *Eucalyptus* into the grid, filling the entire surface. This foliage will define the size and shape of the flower arrangement. **02**

Arrange stems of *Gypsophila* among the *Eucalyptus*. This adds softness and also helps to define the size and shape of the flower arrangement. **03**

Arrange the *Alstroemeria* and spray roses into the grid. Insert the roses in roughly triangular configurations throughout the design to ensure the placements are equidistant. **04**

rose
round

Floral design and photos by Lori McNorton

Coat the green sides of some of the *Magnolia* leaves with rose-gold spray paint. Use a paper towel, cardboard or other barrier to protect the rest of the wreath from overspray. **01**

Tape off the top half of a clear glass vase, and wrap rubber bands in overlapping patterns around the lower half of the vase. **02**

Coat the lower half of the vase with rose-gold spray paint. Then add a light coat of frosted matte spray paint. Carefully remove the tape and rubber bands when the paint is dry. **03**

MATERIALS

Spray roses (*Rosa* spp.); *Eustoma/Lisianthus* blooms and buds; Preserved oak leaves or fresh *Eucalyptus* or English ivy (*Hedera helix*) leaves; Steel grass (*Xanthorrhoea*) or bear grass (*Xerophyllum*); Liquid floral adhesive; Hair comb.

MATERIALS

'Red Naomi' (or similar) red roses (*Rosa* spp.); *Skimmia*; Laurustinus (*Viburnum* spp.); Stem wrap; Florist wire; Narrow satin ribbon in a color of your choice.

MATERIALS

Spray roses (*Rosa* spp.); *Gypsophila*; English ivy (*Hedera helix*) leaves; Hard plastic hairband; Liquid floral adhesive.

01 Run a layer of glue along the top of the comb, and wait for a couple of minutes to allow it to get tacky.

02 Adhere a foundation of leaves to the comb, making sure the teeth are mostly uncovered. Overlap them slightly over the edges of the comb.

03 Glue flowers and additional foliage to the leaf covered comb.

01 Tape two pieces of florist wire together (in pairs) to make a length of about 28 inches. Create a small loop at each end of the taped florist wires.

02 Cut the stems of the flowers and foliage to about 1 inch in length.

03 Insert a wire up the center of each rose stem to give support should the stem snap.

04 Lay the flowers and foliage in a pleasing order, starting and finishing with a piece of foliage.

05 Place the first piece of *Skimmia* to just cover the end of one loop, and join it to the wire with stem wrap. Do this twice so that it is secure.

06 Continue along the wire, adding flowers, interspersing *Skimmia* and laurustinus at regular intervals and finishing with a piece of foliage.

07 Thread a length of the ribbon through each of the two loops so that the circlet can be secured. Cut the ends neatly with dressmaking scissors.

01 Run a line of liquid floral adhesive along the top of the band, and wait for a couple of minutes to allow it to get tacky.

02 Place a few small ivy leaves or other plain leaves on the band so they overlap.

03 Put a dab of glue behind each rose bloom. Wait until the glue is tacky, and then place the flowers at regular intervals along the band.

04 Fill in any gaps with sprigs of *Gypsophila*.

flaunt your flowers

Floral design by Judith Blacklock

Floral design and photo by Lori McNorton. See how-to design and steps on Pages 84–85.

SPRING

Cut a length of yarn to create the hanger for the design. Thread the yarn through the brass tube, and secure with a double knot. Trim excess, and conceal the knot inside the brass tube. **01**

Cut 10 to 15 equal lengths of yarn to create fringe. Fold each yarn length in half, and loop around the brass tube. Pull the ends through the loop until snug. Repeat, and space yarn equal distances across the brass tube. **02**

Starting with the largest branches, determine the shape of the design. Connect two large branches with paper-covered wire at a minimum of two points. **03**

Layer additional branches to echo the desired shape. Secure each branch with paper-covered wire, taking care to conceal binding points. **04**

Add *Magnolia* branches. Secure with paper-covered wire. **05**

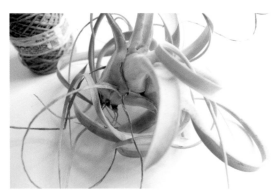

Wrap and twist paper-covered wire carefully around the *Tillandsia bulbosa* and *Tillandsia xerographica*, leaving tails. Attach *Tillandsias* to the branch armature, being mindful of weight distribution. **06**

Add ringneck pheasant feathers, and attach with paper-covered wire. **07**

Create tufts of *Tillandsia usneoides*, thread paper-covered wire through each tuft, and secure with a twist while leaving tails. Fill gaps surrounding the larger *Tillandsia*. Secure the tails to the armature. **08**

Turn the armature over so the back is facing up. Thread a few zip ties through the armature. **09**

Lay the brass tube covered with yarn fringe onto the armature, and secure the two pieces together by securing the zip ties. Trim excess plastic from zip ties. **10**

Hang the design. Trim the yarn fringe to the desired length and shape. **11**

Instruct clients to remove the *Tillandsias* from the design and submerge them in water for a few hours once a week during warm seasons and once or twice a month during cold seasons. They can then reattach the *Tillandsias* to the design after soaking. **12**

modern wreath

MATERIALS

Tillandsia bulbosa, Tillandsia xerographica, Tillandsia usneoides (Spanish moss), *Usnea* lichen branches and *Magnolia grandiflora* (bull bay, Southern *Magnolia*) foliage, brass tube, yarn and zip ties from suppliers of your choice; Kiwi Vine Gold Leaf, Ringneck Pheasant Feathers and Natraj Varnished from **Knud Nielsen Company**; Oasis Bind Wire (Natural) from **Smithers-Oasis North America**.

Floral design and photos by Stacey Carlton, AIFD, EMC

Insert a taped wire through holes in one end of the cuff, and twist it to secure it. This wire will bind the corsage to the cuff. **01**

Insert another taped wire through holes in an opposite section of the cuff, and twist it to secure it. **02**

Wire and tape individual flowers. **03**

Start assembling the corsage by taping together smaller flowers, followed by larger blossoms in the center, and then smaller blooms again. **04**

Lay the corsage atop the cuff, and wire it to the cuff with the taped wires. **05**

Finish by gluing *Allium* and *Nerine* blossoms and raspberry leaves into the corsage with liquid floral adhesive. **06**

new take on a wrist corsage

MATERIALS
Wrist cuff from **Forever 21**; übermatte Color Finish spray (Crema) from **Design Master Color Tool**; Oasis Floral Adhesive, Oasis Florist Wire (24 gauge) and Floratape Stem Wrap from **Smithers-Oasis Company**; sharp clippers; spray roses (*Rosa* spp.), pincushion flowers (*Scabiosa* spp.), white and terra-cotta Persian buttercups (*Ranunculus asiaticus*), *Allium* spp., Guernsey lilies (*Nerine sarniensis*), raspberry leaves (*Rubus* spp.)

Floral design by Susan McLeary • Photos by Amanda Dumouchelle

MATERIALS

Ranunculus asiaticus (Persian buttercups) and *Myrtus* spp. (myrtle) from **Mellano & Company**; assorted succulents; Aspen Yellow, Robin's Egg and Coral Bright Colortool sprays, Delphinium Blue Just For Flowers spray and Salmon übermatte spray from **Design Master Color Tool**; 4-inch clear vinyl basket liner from **Curtis Wagner Plastics Corp.**; Oasis Floral Foam MaxLife and Lomey Corsage Pins from **Smithers-Oasis North America**; rain boots; bubble wrap.

Paint a trio of varied succulents with bright color sprays, giving each the look of a colorful flower. **01**

Insert trios of pink-headed corsage pins into the center of a rosette-form succulent to mimic a bloom's pistil. **02**

Arrange the trio of succulents into soil in a vinyl basket liner. Fill each boot two-thirds full with bubble wrap to support the basket liner in one and a block of floral foam in the other. **03**

blooming boots

Floral design and photos by Lori McNorton • Flowers and other considerations provided by

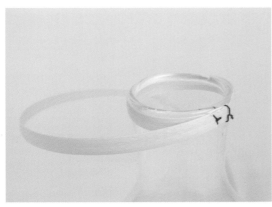

Make a ring of flat cane to fit the outer edge of the opening for your container. **01**

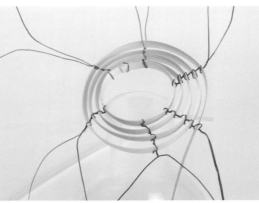

Cut six pieces of paddle wire about 16 inches in length. Evenly around the ring, wrap a wire around the flat cane at the halfway point of the wire, and twist several times. **02**

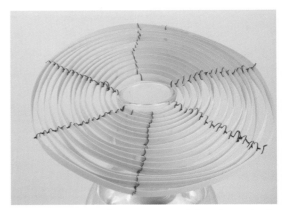

Start weaving flat cane around the wires using a spiral *tatami* technique until the desired size for the armature is achieved. Be sure to always twist the wire exactly the same number of times in order to maintain the shape and symmetry of the armature. **03**

Glue *Salix viminalis* sticks around the armature using your glue gun. **04**

Pierce *Sedum morganianum* leaves on each stick, and secure them with floral adhesive. **05**

modern
spin

MATERIALS

Ranunculus asiaticus (Persian buttercups), *Tulipa* 'Dream Touch' (double peony-flowered tulips), *Eucalyptus gunnii* (cider gum), *Achillea millefolium* (yarrow), *Salix matsudana* 'Tortuosa' (curly willow), *Salix viminalis* (dried basket willow), *Sedum morganianum* (burro's tail), glass container, flat cane, paddle wire, glue gun, glue sticks liquid floral adhesive.

Floral design by Leopoldo Gómez

rose gold wreath

MATERIALS
'Sahara' roses (*Rosa* spp.) from **Eufloria Flowers**; 'Jana' spray roses (*Rosa* spp.) from **California Pajarosa Floral**; pomegranates from **Knud Nielsen Company**; glass ornaments (Pale Pink Pearl) from **The Whitehurst Company**; Rose Gold Premium Metals spray and überfrost spray from **Design Master Color Tool**; Rose Silk ribbon from **Lion Ribbon Company**; wreath from **The Magnolia Company**; Holders and Bind Wire (Green) from **Smithers-Oasis North America**; Patrician Disk Floating Candles from **Candle Artisans**; *Sedum*; vase.

Floral design and photos by Lori McNorton

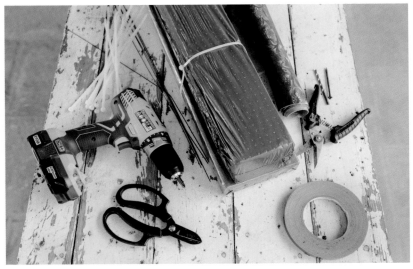

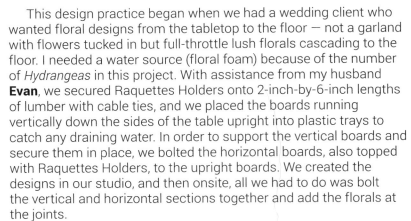

This design practice began when we had a wedding client who wanted floral designs from the tabletop to the floor — not a garland with flowers tucked in but full-throttle lush florals cascading to the floor. I needed a water source (floral foam) because of the number of *Hydrangeas* in this project. With assistance from my husband **Evan**, we secured Raquettes Holders onto 2-inch-by-6-inch lengths of lumber with cable ties, and we placed the boards running vertically down the sides of the table upright into plastic trays to catch any draining water. In order to support the vertical boards and secure them in place, we bolted the horizontal boards, also topped with Raquettes Holders, to the upright boards. We created the designs in our studio, and then onsite, all we had to do was bolt the vertical and horizontal sections together and add the florals at the joints.

This technique was a game-changing design for us. Walking into a venue and placing the horizontal designs on each table and attaching them to two upright boards is infinitely easier then bringing in multiple small designs and trying to piece them together on site. Now we design on 2-by-6s all the time. We create all of our mantelpieces and significant one-sided designs on 2-by-6s.

cascading centerpiece

MATERIALS
Raquettes Holders from **Smithers-Oasis North America**; 6-inch Designer Trays from **Syndicate Sales**; cable ties and 2-inch-by-6-inch lumber from home improvement store or hardware store.

Floral design by Holly Heider Chapple • Photos by Emily Gude

Tape together the bottom portion of 14 pieces of wire with stem wrap. **01**

Twist pairs of wires downward at a 90 degree angle. **02**

Start weaving the wires using a "chicken wire" technique. **03**

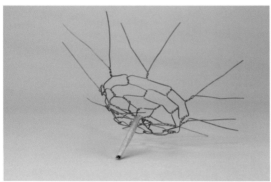

Continue weaving the wires, creating a bowl shape with the wires. **04**

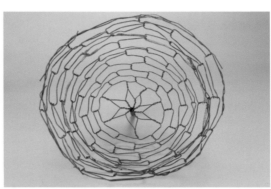

Using stem wrap, tape another wire to the end of each of the original 14 wires to extend the length in order to create the right size armature that can hold all of the orchid plants. **05**

Cut out the center of the armature to remove the handle. Bend three of the open-ended wires downward, and hot-glue them into the wooden drawer pulls underneath the armature. **06**

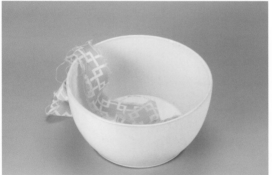

Prepare a mixture of 75 percent white glue and 25 percent water. Cut strips of fabric approximately 1 inch to 2 inches thick, dip them into the glue/water mixture and set them aside to dry. **07**

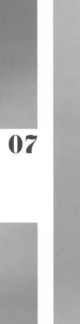

When the strips of fabric are dry, weave some of them throughout the armature, and hot-glue additional strips to the inside and outside of the armature to create a nice texture and combination of the fabrics. Once the "fabric basket" is complete, glue a plastic bag to the inside of the container to protect the fabric from moisture when the plants get watered. **08**

handicrafted
basket

MATERIALS

Phalaenopsis spp. (moth orchid) plants, moss, fabric (assorted colors and/or patterns), wood drawer pulls, 28 pieces of wire (18 gauge or heavier), Floratape Stem Wrap from **Smithers-Oasis North America**, white glue, glue gun, glue sticks, plastic bag.

Floral design by Leopoldo Gomez

Using a flexible ruler and the line grid on a cutting mat as a guide, trace an elongated oval shape onto lightweight cardboard, and cut it out. This will be the template for the base. **01**

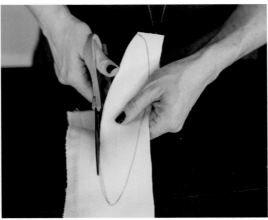

Place the oval cardboard template onto the vinyl fabric, trace the shape, and cut it out. **02**

Insert an eyelet into either side of the vinyl, at the narrow ends of the oval. Instructions for adding the eyelets are included in each kit. **03**

Thread a length of your favorite ribbon through each eyelet to create a pair of ties for the sash. **04**

Remove the flowers' sepals and stems, and add liquid floral adhesive to the flower backs and the vinyl base. Wait about 20 seconds for the adhesive to get tacky. Position the flowers on the vinyl, press firmly and hold for another 15 to 20 seconds. Add larger flowers toward the center, and taper to smaller blooms on the sides. Add flowers and foliages to both sides. **05**

The finished design can be worn as a belt, necklace or crown, using the ribbon ties to secure. To wear the piece as a shoulder corsage, cut off the ribbon ties, and pin the sash in place using two corsage pins — one at the top and one at the bottom of the piece. **06**

flexible fashion

MATERIALS

Scabiosa atropurpurea 'Vanilla Scoop' and 'Fama White' (pincushion flower), *Brunia* spp., *Asclepias* 'Ice Ballet' (swamp milkweed), pearl *Acacia* (*A. podalyriifolia*), *Gomphrena* spp.(globe amaranth), *Ozothamnus diosmifolius* (rice flower), *Nerine sarniensis* (Guernsey lily), Chilean fern and satin ribbon from suppliers of your choice; vinyl fabric (marine or upholstery vinyl) and eyelet kit from fabric or craft store; Oasis Floral Adhesive and Lomey Corsage Pins from **Smithers-Oasis North America**.

Floral design by Susan McLeary • Photos by Amanda Dumouchelle

Place trimmed floral-foam blocks into the container, extending the foam just above the rim of the container. **01**

Arrange roselilies to bisect the center of the design. Press a pencil or dowel into the floral foam to create the insertion points for the callas so that their soft stems are more easily inserted to reach the water source. **02**

Arrange the callas so that they shelter the roselilies and other florals, and shape the stems gently with your hands. Continue arranging more flowers and foliages. **03**

bold and beautiful

MATERIALS

'Isabella' roselilies (*Lilium* spp.), 'Hong Kong' *Iris*, 'Cantor' and 'Rudolph' callas (*Zantedeschia* spp.), 'White Liberstar' tulips (*Tulipa* spp.), 'Sweet Pink' *Kalanchoe* and California bay leaves (*Umbellularia* spp.) from **The Sun Valley Group**; *Phalaenopsis* (moth orchids) from **CosMic Plants**; *Dianthus* spp. from favorite supplier; ZigZag Planter from **Accent Décor**; Oasis Floral Foam Maxlife from **Smithers-Oasis North America**.

Floral design and photos by Lori McNorton

Wire grape hyacinth stems to wood picks, to support the soft stems, and wrap the picks in green stem wrap to hide the mechanics. The wood picks also help the blooms hold their poses in the bouquet. **01**

Wind jasmine vine around the bouquet, wending among the blooms, and tuck the two ends into the center of the bouquet for security. **02**

Wire four lengths of ribbon to a wood pick, tape the wood pick with stem wrap and insert it into the bouquet base to create a quartet of ribbon streamers. If desired, tie loose knots along the lengths of the ribbons to add interest. **03**

MATERIALS
'Charity' and 'Mayra's Rose' garden roses from **Alexandra Farms**; grape hyacinths (*Muscari*), speedwell (*Veronica*) and jasmine (*Jasminum*) from suppliers of your choice; maidenhair fern (*Adiantum*) from **FernTrust**; Double Face Satin ribbons (Vapor #5 and #9) from **Lion Ribbon Company**; Venus Bouquet Holder from **Syndicate Sales**; Stem Wrap from **Milton Adler Company**; wired wood picks from **Premium Wood Picks**.

hint of blue

Floral design and photos by Lori McNorton

Gather all materials – flowers, foliage and hard goods. Clip the pothos leaves from the vine, and cut the spray rose stems short. **01**

Arrange the pothos leaves into the floral-foam heart. Using a length of beaded wire, create a garland around the heart, bunching the wire to create groups of beads. Secure with greening pins. **02**

Arrange the spray rose clusters among the pothos leaves, distributing the rose varieties evenly around the heart. Wind ribbon throughout, securing it with greening pins. **03**

have my heart

MATERIALS
'Pavlova', 'Astral', 'Lovely Lydia' and 'Nemo' spray roses (*Rosa* spp.) from **California Pajarosa Floral**; 'Silver Satin' pothos (*Scindapsus pictus*) plant; 12-inch Oasis Mâché Open Heart and Oasis Mega Beaded from **Smithers-Oasis North America**; Deena ribbon (Pink) from **Lion Ribbon Company**; greening pins from **Syndicate Sales**; butterfly clips.

Floral design and photos by Lori McNorton

MATERIALS

'Eskimo' roses (*Rosa* spp.) from **Virgin Farms Direct**; lemon button fern (*Nephrolepis cordifolia* 'Duffii'), 4-inch pink *Cyclamen* plant; Oasis Bind Wire and 4-inch Single Anchor Water Pick from **Smithers-Oasis North America**; yarn, red wool sheeting and needle felting wool from craft store; bird statue.

Cut three equal-size strips of red wool, with the height equaling that of a water pick or water tube. Arrange three water picks or tubes atop one of the wool strips and two water tubes atop another wool strip. **01**

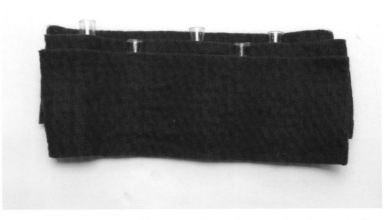

Place one wool strip with water picks or tubes atop the other, so that the picks/tubes are alternating in their placement, and place the third wool strip atop the first two. Experiment with longer wool strips and more water picks/tubes for a larger posy. **02**

Roll the three wool strips together into a bundle, and stand the bundle on its end. Secure the bundle with a wrap of paper-covered wire. **03**

Wrap strips of felting wool around the bundle to conceal the bind wire and add interest and detail. Tie a yarn bow to the wool as a final flourish. Add flower-food solution to the water picks/ tubes, and arrange fresh flowers and foliages into them. **04**

felted
posy

Floral design and photos by Lori McNorton

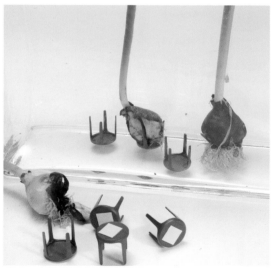

Attach anchor pins, with pins pointing **01** upward, to the clean, dry inner base of the vase using adhesive dashes.

Cradle tulip bulbs into the anchor pins **02** to hold the blooms steady and upright.

Continue nestling bulbs into the anchor **03** pins, and support other tulip bulbs between the pins. *TIP*: Particularly in taller vases, it is easier to add the rock layer as the bulbs are inserted rather than after the tulips are arranged. Add just enough water to cover the roots and reach the bottoms of the bulbs.

singular
blooms

MATERIALS
Tulips on the Bulb (assorted colors) and 'Orange Princess', 'Moscotte' and 'Columbus' cut tulips (*Tulipa* spp.) from **The Sun Valley Group**; Oval Glass Vase from **Floral Supply Syndicate**; Moderne Vase from **Accent Décor**; decorative rocks from **FloraCraft**; Oasis UGlu Adhesive Dashes and Anchor Pins from **Smithers-Oasis North America**.

Floral design and photos by Lori McNorton

MATERIALS

White *Hydrangea* (hortensia) from **The Sun Valley Group**; 'Freedom' roses (*Rosa* spp.) from **Virgin Farms Direct**; seeded *Eucalyptus* from **Mellano & Company**; Queen Anne's lace/bishop's weed *(Ammi majus)*; Levee Vase from **Accent Décor**; Double Hearts large topper from **Floral Supply Syndicate**; Oasis Bullion Wire (Gold) from **Smithers-Oasis North America**.

Gather the container, botanical materials and hard goods. **01**

Encircle the decorative vase with bullion wire in a casual, haphazard fashion, and arrange two stems of seeded *Eucalyptus* into the opening of the vase. Wrap the ends of the bullion wire around the stems to hold the bullion wire in place. **02**

Arrange *Hydrangea* into the vase to form a rounded base for the floral design. **03**

Arrange three roses, ascending in stair-step fashion, and add Queen Anne's lace and the heart accent. **04**

sparkling trio

Floral design and photos by Lori McNorton

Assemble your container, florals and hard goods. **01**

Gently bend the spine of a cast-iron *(Aspidistra)* leaf, and loosely fold the majority of the leaf on a diagonal. **02**

Form a cone shape with the leaf by circling the top of the leaf over the front and around the back. **03**

Secure the cone shape using a plier stapler, with the flat side of the staple on the outside of the leaf. **04**

Place a rose stem through top of the leaf cone and out through the bottom until the rose is nestled inside. **05**

Bind the rose stem and *Aspidistra* leaf stem together with paper-covered wire. Repeat this process with as many roses as you wish, and arrange the rose/leaf duos into an arrangement, a bud vase or a bouquet. **06**

modern love

MATERIALS

'Freedom' roses (*Rosa* spp.) from **Virgin Farms Direct**; *Aspidistra* leaves from **FernTrust**; Oasis Bind Wire (Natural) from **Smithers-Oasis North America**.

Floral design and photos by Stacey Carlton, AIFD, EMC

MATERIALS

Iron-cross *Begonia* leaves or multicolored rex *Begonia* leaves; *Calathea* leaves; *Ranunculus* (Persian buttercup buds); checkered lily (*Fritillaria meleagris*) blooms; assorted *Sedum* (stonecrop) and other succulents; *Eucalyptus* seedpods; witch hazel seedpods (*Hamamelis* spp.); Australian fern; Oasis Floral Adhesive; stiletto shoe

Glue the *Begonia* leaves onto the sides of the shoes. **01**

Glue the *Calathea* leaves onto the heels and soles of the shoes as well as inside the shoes. **02**

Glue the other botanical materials around the opening of the shoes. **03**

botanical shoe

Floral design by Françoise Weeks • Photos by Gwendolyn Severson

Place a soaked block of floral foam into the urn, extending an inch or two above the rim of the container.

01

Establish the center and side points of the triangular shape with leatherleaf fern fronds placed vertically and horizontally, and fill in between those points with more leatherleaf. This greenery will define the size and triangular shape of the arrangement.

02

Wire a ribbon bow to a wood pick, and tuck it into the base of the design before adding the flowers; this makes the bow integral to the design and not appear as an afterthought. Arrange the line flowers first, followed by the form flowers to fill out the triangular shape.

03

classic
sympathy
spray

MATERIALS

'Roberta' roselilies (*Lilium* spp.), 'Casa Blanca' *Iris* and California bay leaves (*Umbellularia*) from **The Sun Valley Group**; spray carnations (*Dianthus caryophyllus nana*), larkspurs (*Consolida* spp.) and leatherleaf fern (*Rumohra* spp.) from favorite suppliers; Black Pearl Millennium Urn from **Vacuum Orna Metal**; Pewter Ombre Ribbon from **Lion Ribbon Company**; Atlantic Brand Waterproof Tape and Oasis Floral Foam Maxlife from **Smithers-Oasis North America**; wood pick.

Floral design and photos by Lori McNerton

MATERIALS
'Adventure' *Gerbera*, 'Donna' hybrid tea roses and 'Babe' spray roses (*Rosa* spp.) from **Sunburst Farms**; 'Safari Sunset' *Leucadendron* and willow *Eucalyptus* from **Resendiz Brothers Protea Growers**; red huckleberry (*Vaccinium* spp.) and salal tips (*Gaultheria shallon*) from **FernTrust**; bamboo (*Bambusa vulgaris*) from **Knud Nielsen Company**; orange *Gladioli*; No. 9 Soft Gold Anisha Wire Edge ribbon from **Lion Ribbon Company**; 6" Moss ECOssentials Cylinder, 1/4" Oasis Green Waterproof Tape and Oasis Floral Foam Maxlife from **Smithers-Oasis North America**.

Arrange three *Gladiolus* in the center and slightly to the left of center in the container, at staggered heights. Then arrange three *Gerbera* to the right of center, also at staggered heights. **01**

Place two stems of bamboo on the left side of the arrangement, on a slight diagonal. Tie a length of ribbon to the bamboo in an artful manner, such as that shown. **02**

Arrange a cluster of spray roses on the lower right side of the design, a cluster of hybrid tea roses on the lower left side, and a cluster of *Leucadendron* in the front of the composition, where a bow might normally be placed. Finish by arranging foliages. **03**

tradition with a twist

Floral design and photos by Lori McNorton

01 Choose coordinating materials – bracelet, leaves, ribbon, gems, etc.

01 Wire a rose stem and a fresh *Ruscus* leaf using the hairpin wiring method.

02 Glue three fabric leaves to the plastic platform on the jeweled floral bracelet with liquid floral adhesive.

Make an eight-loop bow with No. 3 ribbon, and glue the bow atop the leaf base on the bracelet with liquid floral adhesive.

02 Tape the wired rose stem and the wired leaf with stem wrap.

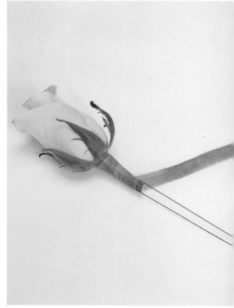

03 Glue a rose into the center of the bow, and then glue fresh foliage, bits of pepperberry and succulents, *Kalanchoe* blossoms, rolled rose petals and gem sprays into the bow, surrounding the rose.

03 Tape the leaf to the back of the rose with stem wrap, and cut the stem to the desired length. Glue *Kalanchoe* blooms and a gem spray to the base of the rose with liquid floral adhesive. Insert the taped boutonnière stem firmly into decorative conical boutonnière "holder." You can secure the stem into the holder with a dab of liquid floral adhesive or an adhesive dot, if you desire.

basic doesn't mean boring

MATERIALS

'Clear Ocean' hybrid tea roses (*Rosa* spp.) from **Sunburst Farms**;
cut *Kalanchoe* from **The Sun Valley Group**; California pepperberry (*Schinus molle*) and succulents from suppliers of your choice; Israeli *Ruscus* from **FernTrust**; Bright Lights Flower Bracelet, Explosion starburst gem, Wowza Dazzle gem pin and Sterling Rock It Boutonnière holder from **Fitz Design**; Mesh Classic Wire Edge ribbon from **Reliant Ribbons Bows & Trims**; Glitter Leaves, Oasis Floral Adhesive and Floratape Stem Wrap from **Smithers-Oasis North America**.

Floral designs and photos by Lori McNorton

Place each flower stem into a water tube filled with flower-food solution. **01**

Layer a large square of tissue paper atop an equal-size square of kraft paper, with the tissue extending slightly beyond the kraft paper. Lay a bed of foliage onto the tissue paper, with the tips angled toward a corner of the papers. **02**

Layer flowers atop the foliage, placing the blooms in a progressively widening stair-step pattern, to create a triangular form. **03**

Fold the bottom corner of the paper square up and over the stems of the flowers, making sure the stems are fully covered. Fold each of the two side corners toward the center of the bouquet, folding about one-third of the way across. **04**

Tie the base of the bouquet with a ribbon to secure the blooms and the wrap. **05**

Fold down the front corners of the wrap, and fluff the tissue paper around the bouquet to create a collared effect. **06**

master beautiful
bouquet wraps

MATERIALS

Alstroemeria (Peruvian lilies) from **Mellano & Company**; *Limonium* spp. from **Ball SB**; leatherleaf fern (*Rumohra* spp.), salal tips (*Gaultheria shallon*) and myrtle (*Myrtus* spp.) from **FernTrust**; carnations (*Dianthus caryophyllus*); *Chrysanthemum*; #9 Brown-striped Faux Burlap Ribbon from **Harvest Import**; brown kraft paper and tissue paper from **Nashville Wraps**; Aquaplus and Aquatubes from **Syndicate Sales**.

Floral design and photos by Lori McNorton

Tie a multiloop bow with two coordinating ribbons. Wire the bow to a wood pick, tape the wood pick with stem wrap (so it won't wick water from the arrangement) and insert into the arrangement. Wend several tails through the design itself for added interest.

Tangiers Pale Peach #9
Double Face Satin Palomino #9

Knot two double-faced satin ribbons at the base of a cylinder vase. Wrap the tails around either side of the vase, meeting in the back, twisting around each other and returning the ends to the front of the vase. Repeat the twist, and wrap the tails to the back of the vase. Keep weaving the ribbons together until you reach the top of the vase. Finish with a knot, and leave the tails long. Secure the knots – and twists if needed – with adhesive dots or double-sided tape.

Double Face Satin Dusty Blue #9
Double Face Satin Azurite #9

Layer three coordinating ribbons to form a bow. Vary the patterns, colors, finishes and textures for the most impact while complementing the flowers the bow will accompany. After tying the bow, gently pull the loop layers apart to add volume and better highlight each individual ribbon. Begin arranging the flowers on all sides of the bow (the bow serves as an armature), working in a circular fashion to create a hand-tied bouquet, with the bow and tails forming its central feature.

Delilah Wire-edge Multi #40
Frayed Anisha (Franisha) Gold #40
Blended Wire-edge Pink/Orange #9

beribboned beauties

Floral designs by Deborah De La Flor, AIFD, PFCI • Photos by Mel Englander • Ribbons provided by

LION™

Maker Apron from Virginia Dare Dress Company

MATERIALS

Persian buttercups (*Ranunculus asiaticus*), 'Silver Mikado' spray roses (*Rosa* spp.), larkspurs (*Consolida* spp.), silver-dollar *Eucalyptus*, seeded *Eucalyptus*, plumosa fern (*Asparagus setaceus*), *Viburnum* berries, blackberries (*Rubus* spp.) and lily-of-the-valley bush (*Pieris japonica*) from **DVFlora**; beautyberry (*Callicarpa americana*) from **Hope Flower Farm**; ribbon from **Honey Silks & Co.**; Oasis Floral Adhesive from **Smithers-Oasis North America**; chenille stems and bracelets from suppliers of your choice.

01 Shape chenille stems into small floret--like loops. Wrap several of looped chenille stems onto the bracelet – more loops for heavier flower concentration, fewer loops for lighter flower content. Secure the looped chenille stems in place with a dab of liquid floral adhesive, if desired.

02 Tie short strips of ribbon onto the bracelet at the junctures where the looped chenille stems are attached. This, too, will help secure the looped chenille stems in place.

03 Glue flowers, foliages, berries and other botanicals of you choice onto the looped chenille stem bases with liquid floral adhesive.

bedecked
bangles

Floral design by Holly Heider Chapple • Photos by Rebekah J. Murray • Flowers and other considerations provided by **DVFLORA** *We Deliver Freshness*

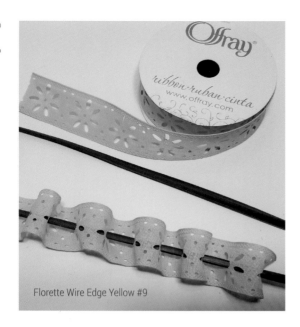

Florette Wire Edge Yellow #9

spring sherbet

Thread stems of lily grass through the holes in lengths of fancy die-cut ribbon in an undulating, wavy manner, to create flirty ribbon adornments. Insert the beribboned greenery throughout your finest, funnest arrangements.

Florette Wire Edge Mint #9
April Pastel #3
Dory Wire Edge Aqua/White #9
Breeze Wire Edge Pink/Blue #9

a-tisket, a-tasket

Weave an assortment of coordinating ribbons in various colors, patterns and widths horizontally through the "netting" of a wire basket. Secure the ends with adhesive dashes in the same locations on one side of the basket. Place a container or liner into the basket, in which to arrange the flowers.

Summery Wire Edge Lavender #9
Franisha Silver #40

lenten thicket

Layer lengths of two ribbons of differing widths, colors and patterns atop one another, with the narrower ribbon on top. Secure the ribbons to each other with adhesive dashes placed every 6 to 8 inches. Midway between each adhesive placement, scrunch the two ribbons, and secure each cinch with the wire on a wired wood pick. Insert the wood picks into the floral foam, at the rim of the container – casually and haphazardly – to create a disordered yet artful base of ribbon around the base of the arrangement and even the container.

easter parade of ribbons

Floral design by Deborah De La Flor, AIFD, PFCI • Photos by Mel Englander • Ribbons provided by

LION™

Cut rose stems short, leaving about 1 inch or less of stem. **01**

Pierce a floral wire through the base of the bloom (calyx), and wrap this wire around the calyx. Leave the other end of the wire long to create a new "stem." **02**

Wrap the base of the rose and the length of the wire with stem wrap. **03**

Arrange a variety of foliage through the openings in the cage to create the beginning outline of the bouquet. **04**

Then arrange the florals, using the cage to help support the bouquet's large size while maintaining a hand-tied look. **05**

Bind the stems just below the cage with waterproof tape. **06**

Gather ribbons of different colors, widths and lengths, and fold each length in half. Secure them together in the center (at the folds) with a corsage pin. **07**

Wrap a length of a wide ribbon around the binding point of the bouquet. **08**

Pin the bundle of ribbon tails into the ribbon-bound binding point. **09**

garden romance

MATERIALS

Persian 'Amaretto' hybrid tea roses and 'Juliet' garden roses (*Rosa* spp.), peonies (*Paeonia lactiflora*), Persian buttercups (*Ranunculus asiaticus*), carnations (*Dianthus caryophyllus*), stock (*Matthiola incana*), speedwell (*Veronica* spp.), lily-of-the-valley bush (*Pieris japonica*), jasmine vine (*Jasminum* spp.), privet berries (*Ligustrum* spp.), blackberries (*Rubus* spp.), heavenly bamboo (*Nandina domestica*) and plumosa fern (*Asparagus setaceus*) from **DVFlora**; ribbons from **Honey Silks & Co.**; Holly Heider Chapple 6" Egg (cage) from **Syndicate Sales**; Oasis Waterproof Tape, Floratape Stem Wrap and Oasis Florist Wire from **Smithers-Oasis North America**.

Floral design by Holly Heider Chapple • Photos by Rebekah J. Murray • Flowers and other considerations provided by **DVFLORA**
We Deliver Freshness

Crumple a section of floral mesh, and spray it thoroughly with a clear-coat finish. Allow the coating to dry overnight, and press the mesh into the base of a bubble bowl. Fill the bowl with properly prepared flower-food solution. **01**

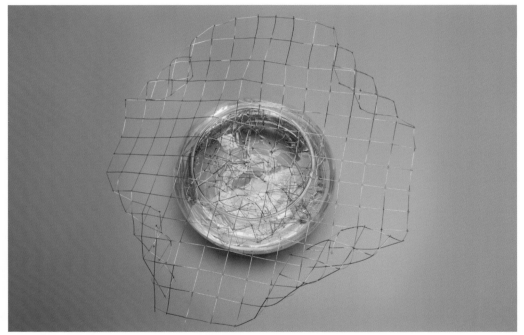

Place a square of floral mesh over the opening of the bowl, extending beyond the bowl's opening by several inches and curling the edges to create a "collar." **02**

Arrange first the *Gypsophila* and then the blooms **03** into a rounded design, using the mesh as a supportive armature.

clean and green

MATERIALS

"Coconut' daisy spray *Chrysanthemum* and 'Country' button spray *Chrysanthemum* from **Rio Specialty Flowers**; 'New Love' *Gypsophila* from **Malima Ecuador**; thoroughwax (*Bupleurum* spp.) from **Mellano & Company**; Floral Mesh (silver) from **Smithers-Oasis North America**; Design Master Clear Finish from **Design Master Color Tool**; 8-inch Bubble Bowl from **Syndicate Sales**.

Floral design and photos by Lori McNorton

Spray interior of wood bowl with Rust-Oleum LeakSeal to create a waterproof barrier, and let the coating dry overnight. **01**

Wrap a wire wreath form with wool felt, paper-covered wire and metallic wire. **02**

Place a pin frog and rocks inside the bowl, fill with properly prepared flower-food solution, and set the wrapped wreath atop the bowl. **03**

Arrange floral materials into the bowl, using the pin frog and rocks to secure the blooms. **04**

making
therounds

MATERIALS

Spray roses (*Rosa* spp.), spray carnations (*Dianthus caryophyllus nana*), Green Trick *Dianthus* (*D. barbatus*), sea holly (*Eryngium* spp.); Oasis Bind Wire (Green), Oasis Bullion Wire (Apple Green) and Oasis Midollino Sticks (Apple Green) from **Smithers-Oasis North America**; 12-inch wire *wreath form; 12-inch wood bowl; river rocks; wool felt; pin frog.*

Floral design by Yoli LaGuerre, AIFD, EMC

Place a band of painter's tape around the **01** middle of a pitcher and lower handle. Spray the lower portion of the pitcher and handle with übermatte spray in a color of your choice to create a custom two-tone container.

Place a few adhesive dashes around the **02** center of the pitcher and lower portion of the handle, along the line of color demarcation, and wrap several rows of bakers twine around the pitcher and handle to add texture and dimension to the surface. Hot-glue permanent botanical blooms to the band of bakers twine.

Design a spiral hand-tied bouquet with flowers **03** of your choice. *Hydrangeas* are used in this bouquet to create an armature through which the other flower stems are arranged. Tie off the bouquet with paper-covered wire, cut the stems to the appropriate length and place the bouquet into the pitcher.

pitcher
perfect

MATERIALS

'Pre-Intenzz' *Gerbera*, 'Cheerio' carnations (*Dianthus caryophyllus*) and blue *Hydrangea* from **Sunburst Farms**; stocks (*Matthiola incana*) and 'Green Ball' *Dianthus* (*D. barbatus*) from **Ball SB**; White Ceramic Pitcher from **Dependable Packaging Solutions**; Mint Green Mom/Message Porcelain Mug from **burton + BURTON**; übermatte Spray (Sprout) from **Design Master Color Tool**; Green Bakers Twine from **Lion Ribbon Company**; Oasis Bind Wire and UGlu Adhesive Dashes from **Smithers-Oasis North America**.

Floral design and photos by Lori McNorton

MATERIALS

'Quicksand' and 'Earl Grey' hybrid tea roses and 'White Majolika' spray roses (Rosa spp.), *Dahlia* 'Cafe au Lait', *Matthiola incana* (stock), *Tweedia caerulea/ Oxypetalum caeruleum*, *Gardenia jasminoides* (cape jasmine), *Eryngium maritimum* (sea holly), *Eucalyptus polyanthemos* (silver-dollar gum), *Olea* spp. (olive branch), *Senecio cineraria/ Jacobaea maritime* (dusty miller) from **Flower Farm**; #9 Double Face Satin (Vapor), #9 Double Face Satin (Dusty Blue) and #9 Satin Grosgrain (Dusty Blue) from **Lion Ribbon Company**; Just for Flowers Transparent Flower Dye (Delphinium Blue) from **Design Master Color Tool**; 6" Pillow from Holly Heider Chapple Exclusively for **Syndicate Sales**.

Create a base for the hand-tied bouquet by arranging stems of silver-dollar *Eucalyptus* and dusty miller through a cage armature. Add other flowers in groupings except for the *Gardenia*, *Tweedia* and *Dahlia*. **01**

Using a hairpin wiring technique, wire and tape all *Gardenia* to create long stems. *Note:* Leave on the plastic collar *(shown here)* or fresh-leaf collar that many *Gardenia* are shipped with until just before they are placed into the bouquet; this helps protect them from possible bruising while being handled. **02**

Tweedia stems require an extra step before arranging them due to the milky substance that "bleeds" from the stems when they are cut and can contaminate the vase water. Before placing *Tweedia* stems into an arrangement, cut each stem on a diagonal, and then singe the stem ends with a flame for just a few seconds. **03**

Arrange *Dahlia* blooms into the bouquet to complete the composition, and place into a decorative vessel. **04**

timeless and sublime

Floral design and photos by Lori McNorton • Sponsored by **flower ❧ farm**
smarter sourcing

footed bowl

Encircle a footed glass bowl with a wide single-face satin ribbon, using a dab of adhesive to hold it in place, if necessary. Tie a narrower complementary ribbon around the bowl, leaving the tails long. Cut a long piece of the same satin ribbon, and tie its center into the existing knot, to create two more tails. Craft a separate bow with tails, and nestle it among the blooms.

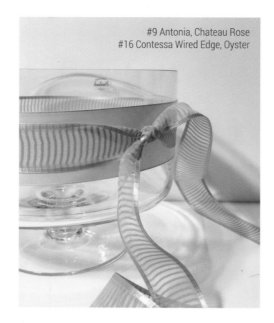

#9 Antonia, Chateau Rose
#16 Contessa Wired Edge, Oyster

posy trio

Tie two lengths of ribbon vertically around (and over the top of) a rectangular container at evenly spaced intervals, dividing the opening of the container into three equal-sized sections. Knot the ribbons atop the opening of the container at one edge of the container, and leave the ribbon tails long. Create two multiloop bows with two different ribbons of the same color. Tie one bow into the knotted section of each ribbon band, using the tails from the bands. Hand-tie three small bouquets, and nestle one into each of the three sections of the container. Where possible, work the ribbon loops among the blooms and vice versa.

#9 Antonia, Dark Shale
#3 Teagan, Dark Shale

chicken wire obelisk

Wire several lengths of two types of ribbon of similar colors to wood picks, and insert them into the floral design. Trim the ribbon tails on the diagonal. To festoon the chicken-wire obelisk topiary, tie lengths of ribbon at the top, and press the ribbon into the wire at intervals to create a woven punctuated-cascade effect.

#9 Antonia, Oyster
#9 Double Face Satin, Palomino

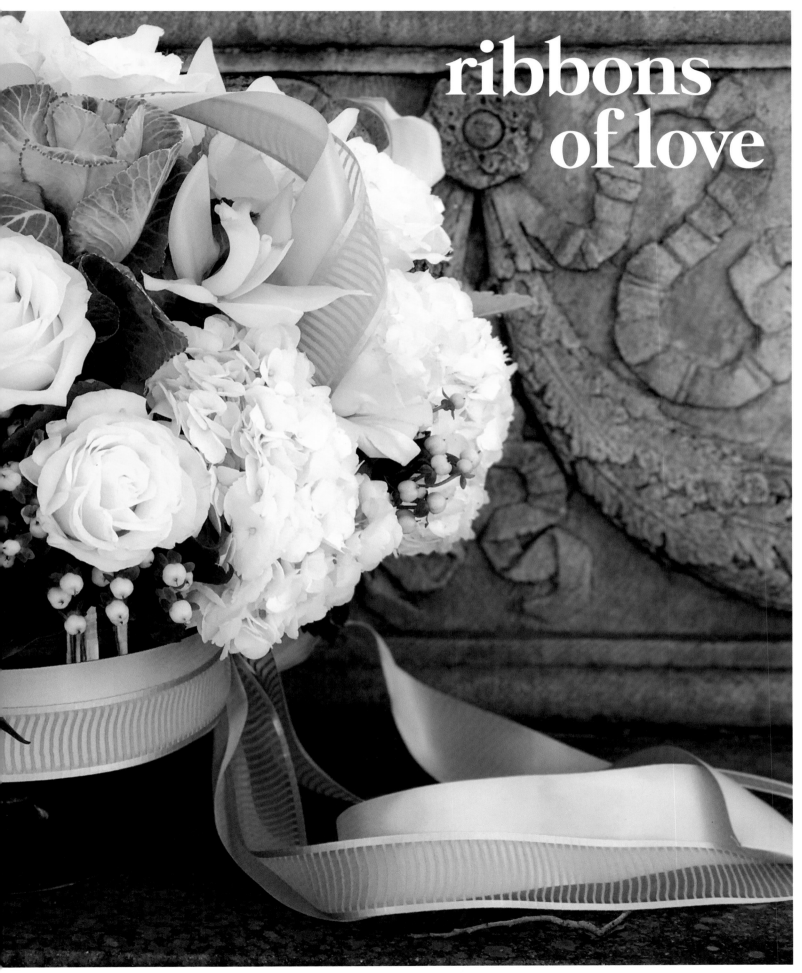

ribbons
of love

Floral design by Deborah De La Flor, AIFD, PFCI • Photos by Mel Englander • Ribbons and other considerations provided by

Measure the height of the space in which you'll hang your tower, to determine the appropriate length of floral mesh. Lay out a length of florist netting (chicken wire), and line the netting with the dried grasses. Curly willow, branches, hardy greenery and even compost scraps will also work. Roll the wire netting around the materials, and secure every 10 to 12 inches with zip ties. **01**

Wind fiber-covered wire through the top of the wire tube, and tie to the ceiling support, or create an appropriate hanging mechanic for your space to suspend the tube. Hang the tube from a strong beam or anchor in the place where it will be displayed before beginning to add the florals. **02**

Cover the wire tube with plumosa fern, and spray paint the fern white. Place the flowers into water picks, and insert the picks into the mesh armature. **03**

hanging garden

MATERIALS

'Phantom Spider' miniature Gerbera (Germini) and 'Ave Maria' Gerbera, 'Santander' Oriental lies (*Lilium* spp.), 'White Winner' Anthurium, 'White VIP' *Eustoma/Lisianthus*, 'Snowflake' spray roses (*Rosa* spp.), *Stephanotis* on the vine and plumosa fern (*Asparagus setaceus*) from **Rosa Flora**; Oasis Florist Netting and Oasis Rustic Wire from **Smithers-Oasis North America**; Aquapics from **Syndicate Sales**; übermatte Spray (Crema) from **Design Master Color Tool**; cable ties from favorite supplier; foraged grasses from garden.

Floral design by Susan McLeary • Photos by Amanda Dumouchelle Photography • Flowers and other considerations provided by **ROSA FLORA** LIMITED *Pride in Every Petal*

Floral design by Holly Heider Chapple. Photo by Rebekah J. Murray. See how-to design and steps on Pages 96–97.

SUMMER

MATERIALS

'Susara' and 'Brenda' *Protea* and 'Baby Blue' *Eucalyptus* from **Resendiz Brothers Protea Growers**; *Berzelia* and *Craspedia* (billy buttons) from **Mellano & Company**; carnations (*Dianthus caryophyllus*) from **Sunburst Farms**; curly willow (*Salix matsudana* 'Tortuosa'); Dixon Pins from **Dixon Products**; sheet moss from **Knud Nielsen Company**; Oasis Maxlife Floral Foam from **Smithers-Oasis North America**; Petite Medallion Planter from **Park Hill Collection**.

Layer moss atop the floral foam in the container, and wind curly willow atop the moss. Form the willow into a few tall loops to extend the design profile. Secure the willow and moss with several Dixon Pins. **01**

Arrange the *Protea* into the floral foam, grouping the blooms so that they fill the entire container. Once dried, these will provide a long-lasting arrangement. **02**

Add carnations, billy buttons, *Berzelia* and *Eucalyptus* to fill in and accent the *Protea*. The carnations can be removed after they fade, but the rest will dry in place. **03**

now
and
later

Floral design and photos by Lori McNorton

Cut six lengths – each approximately 50 inches – of plastic-coated wire. **01**

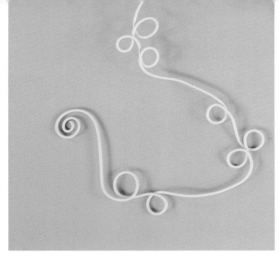

Working with one length at a time, create a spiral at each end using jewelry pliers. Make the first turn of the spiral with the pliers, and continue with your fingers and thumb. Create up to three turns in each spiral. **02**

Using artist paint brush handles in three diameters to wrap the wire around, create circles/loops of different sizes along the length of each wire. **03**

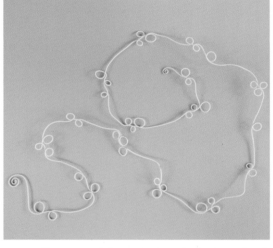

Repeat until the entire length of wire contains these circles/loops. Repeat steps 2 through 4 on each of the remaining lengths of wire. **04**

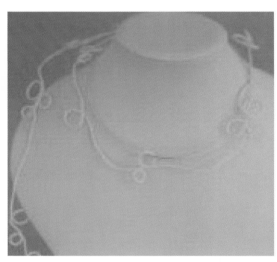

Open the neck ring, and thread one end through the loops on one of the wire lengths, working all the way to the opposite side. Link the other wire lengths onto this first one by interlocking the loops. Continue linking the wires together to create the desired outline, including the cascade at the back of the neck ring. **05**

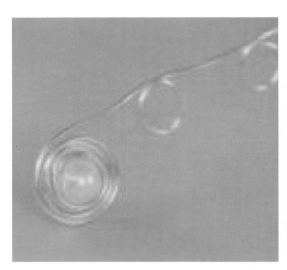

Cut six lengths of thin aluminum wire – approximately 34 inches each – and repeat steps 2 through 4 on each. This time, weave beads onto the wire among the loops as well. **06**

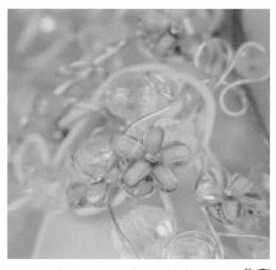

Weave these lengths of beaded aluminum wire into the necklace by interlocking the loops with those of the plastic-coated wire. Glue jewel flowers and additional beads into the framework. **07**

Glue more beads into the wire framework, as desired. As you work, try on the design to ensure it is balanced. **08**

The flowers and small *Sedum* "blooms" rest within the wire loops. To adhere each floret, place liquid adhesive onto a cotton swab, dab the glue around the top and inside of a loop, and adhere the floret into the loop. Continue adding floral materials until the desired look is achieved. **09**

cascading floral wrap

MATERIALS

Agapanthus spp. (lily-of-the-Nile) blossoms, *Saintpaulia* spp. (African violet) blossoms and *Sedum spathulifolium* 'Cape Blanco' from favorite suppliers; Oasis Aluminum Wire and Oasis Floral Adhesive from **Smithers-Oasis North America**; plastic-coated wire (2 mm gauge) from hardware or craft store; jeweled flowers, beads, neck ring and jewelry pliers from jewelry supply or craft store.

Floral design by Wendy Andrade, AIFD, NDSF, FBFA • Photos by Amanda Baker Photography

Choose the floral cage that will best fit atop your container (*Pillow floral cage and Abby Compote shown here*) to provide the armature to brace your foliage and blooms. **01**

Lightly spray the *Hydrangea* blossoms with a pastel color spray to highlight the blooms. Repeat the spray with a slightly darker hue, highlighting just the tips of the blooms for dimensional color. **02**

Choose a variety of complementary foliages, with varying textures and densities, and arrange the stems into the floral cage, crisscrossing in an "X" shape, to create the design's outline. **03**

Arrange the *Hydrangeas* and carnations through the center of the design to create a lush base. Arrange the remaining flowers and foliages at varying depths to fill out the design. **04**

summer bounty

MATERIALS

Garden roses, hybrid tea roses, spray roses (*Rosa* spp.), carnations (*Dianthus caryophyllus*), hortensia (*Hydrangea* spp.), Persian buttercups (*Ranunculus asiaticus*), prairie gentians (*Eustoma/Lisianthus* spp.), parrot tulips (*Tulipa* spp.), loosestrife (*Lysimachia* spp.), snapdragons (*Antirrhinum majus*), pincushion flower (*Scabiosa* spp.), silver-dollar *Eucalyptus*, seeded *Eucalyptus*, plumosa fern (*Asparagus setaceus*), Italian *Ruscus* and *Viburnum* berries from **DVFlora**; Holly Heider Chapple Exclusively for Syndicate Collection Pillow floral cage and Abby compote from **Syndicate Sales**; Hyacinth and Lavender Color Tool sprays from **Design Master Color Tool**.

Floral design by Holly Heider Chapple • Photos by Rebekah J. Murray • Flowers and other considerations provided by **DVFLORA**
We Deliver Freshness

Drill five equidistant holes in the center of a wood plank. **01**

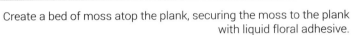

Create a bed of moss atop the plank, securing the moss to the plank with liquid floral adhesive. **02**

Spread floral adhesive onto the base of each succulent, and arrange them among the moss. **03**

Place the plank atop the glass bottles, and glue strands from a string-of-pearls plant into the design. Allow some of the strands to drape over the edges of the plank. **04**

Shave the base of each taper candle to fit the bottle opening. If extra security is needed, secure the candles into the bottles with floral adhesive. **05**

Wire small wood "cookies" onto bullion wire to create a garland. Wind the garland among the succulents, and drape some of the garland off the edges of the plank. **06**

elevated elegance

MATERIALS
Succulents, *Tillandsias*, string-of-pearls (*Senecio rowleyanus*) plant, moss and taper candles from suppliers of your choice; Floral Adhesive and Bullion Wire from **Smithers-Oasis North America**.

Floral design by Svetlana Chernyavsky, AIFD

Place a drop of hot glue onto the container at each location where you would like to adhere the ribbon.

01

Create random loops and swirls, and press the ribbon onto the glue, holding briefly until adhered.

02

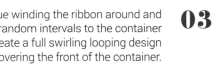

Continue winding the ribbon around and gluing it at random intervals to the container to create a full swirling looping design covering the front of the container.

03

3-dimensional décor

MATERIALS

'Caesar's Palace' Oriental hybrid lilies (*Lilium* spp.) from **The Sun Valley Group**; Carnival ribbon (Black) from **Lion Ribbon Company**; Grab and Go Vase (Black) from **FlowerBox**; hot glue from **Smithers-Oasis North America**.

Floral design and photos by Lori McNorton

MATERIALS

Anthurium andraenum (tail flower), 'Romantic Antike' garden roses (*Rosa* spp.), *Monstera deliciosa* (Swiss cheese plant) leaves, *Alocasia* spp. (elephant's ear) leaves, *Strelitzia reginae* (bird-of-paradise) leaves, *Phoenix roebellenii* (miniature date palm) fronds, palm tree fruit branch and glass cylinder vase from suppliers of your choice; Flat White Colortool Spray, Just for Flowers (Osiana Peach, Petunia Pink and Tiger Lily), and überfrost from **Design Master Color Tool**; Point 'n' Party E-mini 9 4-inch LED light base from **Acolyte Technologies Corp**.

Paint the outside of a clear glass cylinder vase with Tiger Lily Just for Flowers (it works on hard goods, too). After that dries, spray the vase with überfrost. This combination will give the clear glass container a translucent color-frosted finish. **01**

Color fresh foliages of varying shapes and textures by first spraying them lightly with flat white paint. Let dry, and follow with a coat of either Osiana Peach or Pink Petunia Just for Flowers transparent flower dye. After the color spray dries, spray the foliages with überfrost to give them a matte frost finish. **02**

Arrange the flowers and colored foliages into a hand-tied bouquet, place the bouquet into the color-frosted vase, and set the vase on a LED light base. **03**

monotone and multitextural

Floral design by Ian Prosser, AIFD, AAF, PFCI, NDSF • Paints and other considerations provided by

DESIGN
MASTER®

MATERIALS

Leucospermum spp. (pincushions), *Dahlia* spp., cigar *Calathea*, *Craspedia globosa* (billy buttons), *Leucadendron* spp., *Hypericum* spp., *Scabiosa stellata* (starflower pincushions/paper moons) and *Liriope* (lily grass) from suppliers of your choice; Urban Wave Bowl (Slate) from **Syndicate Sales**; apples, potatoes, wood skewers and toothpicks from a supermarket.

01 Create an armature by connecting various sizes and colors of apples and potatoes at varying angles to resemble a molecular structure. Start creating the armature on a table or counter, and then place it atop the opening of the container and continue assembling it there. This will prevent you from having to move it when it is complete.

Arrange flowers into the bowl, through the armature, continuing until you have created the shape and volume you desire. Insert some stems of round botanicals, like billy buttons and starflower pincushions/paper moons, into the potatoes and apples, to continue building the molecular structure. Finish by artfully wending stems of lily grass throughout the design to add rhythm and movement.

molecular
flor-ology

Floral design by Arthur Williams, AIFD, EMC • Photos by Amanda Baker Photography

To hide the bouquet holder, glue moss onto the base of the bouquet holder with liquid floral adhesive. **01**

Glue the scales of a sugar-pine cone onto the moss in an overlapping fashion to mimic their appearance in nature. **02**

Glue a bromeliad leaf around the stem of the bouquet holder, allowing the leaf's pointed end to extend beyond the holder's stem. **03**

Finish the base by gluing the florals, succulents and seedpods around the base of the bouquet stem and around the periphery of the base. **04**

For the bouquet itself, thread a u-shaped piece of 18-gauge floral wire through the bark and the *Tillandsia* leaves, and secure them into the floral foam. **05**

Arrange the foliages, succulents and flowers into the foam, densely packing the bouquet. **06**

forest fantasy

MATERIALS

Air plant (*Tillandsia* spp.); succulents; ornamental kale (*Brassica oleracea*); inch plant /wandering Jew (*Tradescantia zebrina*); *Begonia* leaves; *Sarracenia* spp.; *Kalanchoe* spp.; lady's mantle (*Alchemilla* spp.); Persian buttercups (*Ranunculus asiaticus*): African violets (*Saintpaulia* spp.); *Dianthus* spp.; thistles; *Clematis* spp.; *Berzelia* spp.; *Brunia* spp.; seedpods; bromeliad leaf; ferns; privet (*Ligustrum spp.*); bark; moss; sugar-pine-cone scales; Oasis European Bouquet Holder (Round), Oasis Floral Adhesive and Oasis Florist Wire (18 gauge) from **Smithers-Oasis North America**.

Floral design by Françoise Weeks • Photos by Gwendolyn Severson

01 Band sections of some of the branches/twigs with decorative wire to add a decorative element. Arrange the branches/twigs in an attractive pattern, and glue them together in spots with hot glue. Camouflage visible hot glue spots with a permanent marker.

02 Fill the bowl with sea glass and flower-food solution, and then place the twig armature atop the bowl.

03 Arrange stems of tropical flowers and other botanicals of your choice through the twig armature and into the bowl.

tropical
nouveau

MATERIALS
Miniature *Anthurium andraenum*, *Anemone* spp., *Hypericum* spp., Queen Anne's lace/bishop's weed *(Ammi majus)*, sword fern *(Polystichum* spp)*, Anthurium* foliage, aspen branches *(Populus tremuloides)*; Oasis Bullion Wire (Turquoise) and Oasis All-temp Glue Sticks from **Smithers-Oasis North America**; sea glass, glass bowl.

Floral design by Yoli LaGuerre, AIFD, EMC

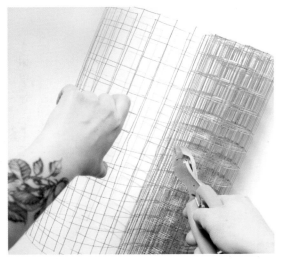

Measure and cut decorative floral mesh. Here, a length of 30 inches is used. **01**

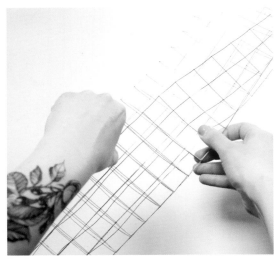

Fold the mesh into thirds lengthwise, or to your desired width, and form into a circular structure. **02**

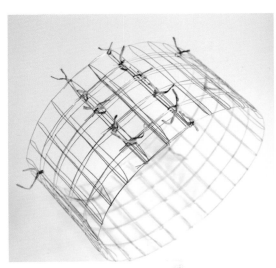

Secure all necessary cross-sections of mesh with paper-covered wire, and trim any excess. **03**

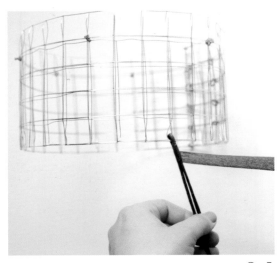

Tape five pieces of heavy-gauge florist wire together with stem wrap. Make six of these thick taped wires. Thread the taped wire through a bottom cross-section of the mesh, fold the wire over, and tape the ends with stem wrap. Repeat multiple times at equal distance. **04**

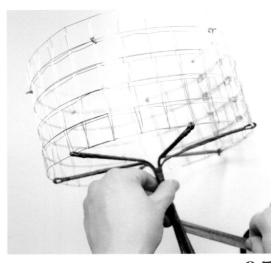

Center and gather all of the taped wires to create a bouquet handle, and tape them together with stem wrap. **05**

Thread Leyland cypress through the mesh, securing with paper-covered wire when necessary. **06**

When the entire mesh ring is covered, spray the foliage with metallic paint. Arrange flowers into the center of gold foliage ring when the paint is dry, to create the bouquet. **07**

Bind the bouquet stems together with paper-covered wire or stem wrap. **08**

Add trimmed and painted Leyland cypress to the underside of the bouquet. Tape all stems together, and finish the bouquet handle as desired. **09**

circle of love

MATERIALS

'Golden Mustard', 'Patience' and 'Princess Miyuki' garden roses (*Rosa* spp.) from **Alexandra Farms**; Lenten roses (*Helleborus orientalis*) and Leyland cypress (*Cupressus × leylandii*) from favorite suppliers; Oasis Bind Wire (Natural), Oasis Floral Mesh (Gold), Oasis Florist Wire and Floratape Stem Wrap from **Smithers-Oasis North America**; Design Master 24KT Pure Gold Premium Metals Metallic Finish from **Design Master Color Tool**; ribbon from favorite supplier.

Floral design and photos by Stacey Carlton, AIFD, EMC

Cover a plastic-foam wreath form with yarn *(shown)*, hair extensions, moss or ribbon. Wrap hair around the wreath form, and pin securely. A firm and unmoving base must be achieved. Work with a hair stylist, if necessary, to ensure a secure base and that the hair is not being pulled from any single point. **01**

Secure the flowers and rolled and folded foliages to the wreath form with corsage pins. Insert rose stems into water tubes, and use the spaces within the structure to conceal the water tubes. **02**

chapeau vivant

MATERIALS

Tail flowers (*Anthurium andraenum*), 'Free Spirit' garden roses (*Rosa* spp.), miniature callas (*Zantedeschia* spp.), *Mokara* orchids, New Zealand flax (*Phormium tenax*), variegated lily grass (*Liriope muscari*), ti leaves (*Cordyline terminalis*), cast-iron leaves (*Aspidistra* spp.), plastic-foam wreath, yarn, corsage pins, water tubes.

Floral design by Arthur Williams, AIFD, EMC, CPF • Photos by Tommy Collier and Aaron Lucy • Colorado Expression Magazine

MATERIALS

CHANDELIER: Wood/Chicken Wire Frame Wall Hanging from **burton + BURTON**; Snapdragons (*Antirrhinum majus*) and statice/sea lavender (*Limonium sinuatum*) from **Rosa Flora**; plumosa fern (*Asparagus setaceus*) from **FernTrust**; Oasis Rustic Wire and Oasis Florist Wire (24 gauge) from **Smithers-Oasis North America**; and übermatte Color Finish (Crema) from **Design Master Color Tool**.

MATERIALS

TABLESCAPE: 4-inch Gold Brushed Tin Double Planter and Floral Sheet Moss from **burton + BURTON**; Madagascar jasmine on the vine (*Stephanotis floribunda*), prairie gentians (*Lisianthus/Eustoma* spp.), snapdragons (*Antirrhinum majus*) and statice/sea lavender (*Limonium sinuatum*) from **Rosa Flora**; 12" Oasis Florist Netting and Oasis Florist Wire (24 gauge) from **Smithers-Oasis North America**.

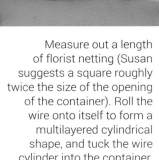

01 Measure out a length of florist netting (Susan suggests a square roughly twice the size of the opening of the container). Roll the wire onto itself to form a multilayered cylindrical shape, and tuck the wire cylinder into the container.

Cut two 5- to 6-inch lengths of florist wire, and secure each to the chicken wire form. These will be used to wire the *Stephanotis* vines into place.

01 Measure two equal lengths of fiber-covered wire with which to hang the wood/chicken-wire frame. The length of the wires will be dependent on the ceiling height and how far above the table you want the finished design to hang. Tie the end of one wire to one corner of the frame and the other wire to the opposite corner of the frame. Secure the frame to a strong, reliable support structure above the table.

02 Attach enameled florist wire to the stems of statice and snapdragons. For each snapdragon, feed about an inch of wire through the flower stem, and bend it to form a hook. Bend the other end of the wire into a hook for hanging the bloom. Wire the statice stems, which are too dense to pierce, by hooking the wire through a joint where a lateral stem meets the main stem and wrapping the wire around each stem to its end. Again, form the other end of the wire into a hook for hanging. Susan used 50 stems of snapdragon and three bunches of statice in creating this floral chandelier. Once all the snapdragons and statice are attached to the frame, lightly dust plumosa fern with white paint, and weave the fern into the wire frame. Susan used two bunches of fern in this chandelier.

03 Wet the moss, and tuck it on top of the wire to conceal the mechanics.

Arrange the *Stephanotis* vine in the planter, securing the vine with the florist wire, as needed.

Pierce *Sedum morganianum* leaves on each stick and secure them with floral adhesive.

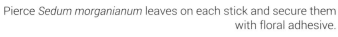 

simply
stunning
setting

Floral design by Susan McLeary • Photos by Amanda Dumouchelle • Sponsored by

burton
+BURTON
theTOTALgift experience®

MATERIALS
Freesia spp. and *Hypericum* spp. from **The Sun Valley Group**; Lenten roses (*Helleborus orientalis*), jasmine vine (*Jasminum* spp.) and English ivy (*Hedera helix*) leaves from favorite suppliers; Emko Non-Wilt Satin Leaves from **Emko**; Lady Fair headband from **The National Ribbon Company**; Oasis Floral Adhesive from **Smithers-Oasis North America**; hair clips.

Trim stems from the satin leaves. Secure one leaf to each hair clip and two leaves to the headband base with liquid floral adhesive. **01**

Adhere fresh leaves and small blooms and *Hypericum* berries to the satin leaves atop each hair clip with liquid floral adhesive. **02**

Place the headband around a cylinder vase to hold it steady for designing. Secure fresh leaves and blooms atop the satin leaves with liquid floral adhesive. **03**

crowning
glory

Floral design and photos by Lori McNorton

Cut a rectangular piece of black felt the length of a standard **01**
bow tie to create the base structure Iron heat-bond tape onto
one edge of the felt, then fold the felt in thirds lengthwise and
iron again so the heat-bond tape secures the edges together.

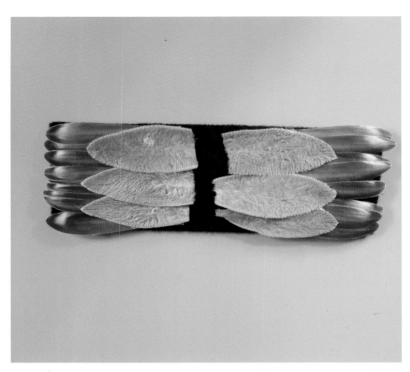

Working from the outside edges of the felt inward and from **02**
top to bottom, adhere individual *Protea* petals to the felt one
row at a time with liquid floral adhesive. Repeat the process,
creating a row lamb's-ear leaves, then add a another row of
smaller *Protea* petals near the center of the bow tie. Repeat
these steps on the other half of the bow tie. Leave a little room
in the center of the piece of felt; this is where you will pull
together the sides with paper-covered wire to create the knot
in the center of the bow tie.

Wrap paper-covered wire around the center of the piece of felt to **03**
create the "knot." Glue small black feathers in the center of the
bow tie, making sure to cover the ends of the *Protea* petals. Next,
glue a small leather strip in the direct center, and secure the ends
in the back with liquid adhesive.

Secure a small curved alligator/beak clip onto the back of the **04**
leather strip so the wearer can attach the bow tie to his shirt.

bow tie in bloom

MATERIALS

Protea hybrid 'Sylvia' from **Resendiz Brothers Protea Growers**; *Stachys byzantina* (lamb's-ears); Oasis Floral Adhesive and Oasis Bind Wire (Brown) from **Smithers-Oasis North America**; black felt, iron-on adhesive, feathers, leather remnants and black curved alligator/beak clip from crafts store.

Floral design and photos by Lori McNorton

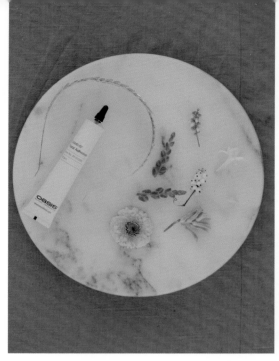

Prepare all of the floral materials by trimming them to size and removing any sepals to create a flush gluing surface. **01**

Apply a fine layer of liquid floral adhesive to the headband. *TIP:* Apply glue to a few inches of the headband at a time, and allow it to stand for a few seconds to get tacky. **02**

Add floral materials, one at a time, starting at one end of the headband. Apply glue to each botanical before pressing it into place on the headband. Start with the tapered and smaller materials, and place larger florals as you work your way to the center of the headband. *TIP:* Trim the "shaft" of the *Stephanotis* blooms so you can tuck them fully into the design. **03**

BOUTONNIÈRE:
Prepare the *Stephanotis* blooms with Stay Fresh *Stephanotis* Stems. Gather the wired stems, a nice selection of buds on the vine and tendrils, and arrange them as you would a tiny bouquet. Form loops with the tendrils, if desired. Secure the binding point of the piece with waterproof tape or stem wrap. Choose an appropriately sized *Stephanotis* leaf, and secure it around the binding point with liquid adhesive. Glue a corsage magnet to the back of the leaf "band."

Glue unopened *Stephanotis* buds into the centers of the *Stephanotis* blooms. **04**

Allow the piece to rest for about 25 minutes to let the glue set. **05**

MATERIALS

BOUTONNIÈRE: *Stephanotis floribunda* on the vine (Madagascar jasmine) from **Rosa Flora**; Stemsons Stay Fresh Stephanotis Stems, Oasis Waterproof Tape (Green) and Lomey Corsage Magnets from **Smithers-Oasis North America**.

petal passion and panache

MATERIALS

HEADBAND: *Gerbera jamesonii* 'Kermit' (miniature Africa daisy), *Stephanotis floribunda* on the vine (Madagascar jasmine), *Antirrhinum majus* (snapdragon) tips, *Angiozanthos* spp. (kangaroo paws), *Symphoricarpos albus* (snowberries) and *Pieris japonica* (lily-of-the-valley bush) from **Rosa Flora**; Oasis Floral Adhesive from **Smithers-Oasis North America**; metal headband from **Claire's**.

Floral design by Susan McLeary • Photos by Amanda Dumouchelle Photography • Sponsored by ROSA*f*LORA LIMITED *Pride in Every Petal*

01 Place an elongated "wadded cage" of floral netting (chicken wire) atop a 2" x 4" board cut to your desired length, and secure the wire to the sides of the board with a staple gun, wire and screws, or other method of your preference.

02 Glue a semicircular piece of wood to the underside of each end of the board, further securing each piece to the board with a wood screw, if desired. Each half-round piece of wood should be half the diameter of the opening in the top of the metal stands.

03 Arrange stems of foliage into the floral netting, with salal/lemonleaf as the base layer. Camouflage the mechanics with your initial greenery insertions. *NOTE:* This design has no blooming botanicals, so no water source is required; however, if you choose to add flowers, place them into water tubes or incorporate floral foam into the base mechanic.

04 Continue arranging other foliages with varying colorations, leaf sizes, textures, etc.

05 Add the most expensive, unusual and/or draping foliages at the end, to better showcase them and to cascade downward, creating movement in the static design.

italian pergola inspiration

MATERIALS & TOOLS

Salal/lemonleaf (*Gaultheria shallon*), *Camellia japonica*, variegated Japanese mock orange (*Pittosporum tobira*), Italian *Ruscus* (*R. aculeatus*), olive tree foliage (*Olea europaea*), plumosa fern (*Asparagus setaceus*), smilax (*Asparagus asparagoides*), hanging votives and battery-operated lights from **DV Flora**; 45" Harlow Stand from **Accent Décor**; 24KT Pure Gold Premium Metals Metallic Finish from **Design Master Color Tool**; taper candles from **Vance Kitira**; Florist Netting from **Syndicate Sales**; Tablecloth and runner from **Honey Silks & Co.**; Maker Apron from **Virginia Dare Dress Company**.

Floral design by Holly Heider Chapple • Photos by Rebekah J. Murray • Sponsored by **DV FLORA** *We Deliver Freshness*

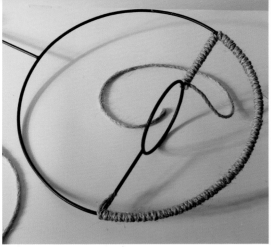

Wrap a hanging metal container with sisal rope, leaving exposed the metal ring that holds the terra-cotta pot. Next add sisal rope accents to the bottom of the clay pot. The rope will give the hanging container a natural texture to complement the organic feel of the floral composition. **01**

Fully hydrate a block of floral foam, and place it securely into the terra-cotta pot. Leave an inch or two of foam above the rim of the pot. **02**

MATERIALS

Zantedeschia spp. 'Garnet Glow' (miniature callas), *Lisianthus/Eustoma* spp. (prairie gentian), *Lilium* 'Party Diamond' (LA hybrid lily) and *Brassica oleraceae* (ornamental kale) from **The Sun Valley Group**; *Antirhhinum majus* (snapdragon) and *Rosa* spp. (hybrid tea roses) from **Fresca Farms**; *Eucalyptus polyanthemos* (silver dollar gum), *Olea europaea* (olive tree foliage) and *Ruscus aculeatus* (Italian *Ruscus*) from **Flower Farm**; *Chrysanthemum* and *Salix matsudana* 'Tortuosa' (curly willow) from favorite suppliers; Plantie Hanging Vase from **Accent Décor**; UGlu Adhesive Strips, Oasis Bind Wire (Natural) and Oasis Floral Foam Maxlife from **Smithers-Oasis North America**; 1/4" Sisal Wire Rope (Brown) from **Harvest Import**.

Artfully arrange foliage into the floral foam, establishing the boundaries of the design. The light and airy foliage chosen for this design creates movement without compromising important negative space. **03**

Wire and tape the stems of two different sized clusters of grapes. Place the larger bunch to cascade below the bottom of the circle, and secure the smaller bunch to the top of the circle with paper-covered wire. **04**

Arrange callas into the design. Secure each calla head at the top of the circular structure with paper-covered wire. **05**

Arrange other botanicals to complete the design. **06**

Suspend the finished design from any support structure indoors or out. **07**

all'aperto influence

Floral design and photos by Lori McNorton

Using pan-melt glue, adhere **01** Midnight Floral Foam bricks onto a 1″ x 4″ board, the length of which fits the space to be decorated. If desired, lightly rub seams with another brick of Midnight Foam to "sand away" seam lines and make the foam appears as one continuous unit. Soak floral foam in a tall trash can or similar container until it is thoroughly saturated (including the center). Midnight Floral Foam will turn from dark gray to black when wet.

Arrange foliage, branches and **02** flowers into the floral foam, starting at one end of the board. Plan your stem insertions before making them to avoid creating too many holes in the foam. If you make holes in the foam that you cannot cover with foliages or flowers, carefully fill them with scraps of foam. Incorporate plenty of negative space into your design, allowing the Midnight Floral Foam to serve as a backdrop for the floral materials and to create interest in the design.

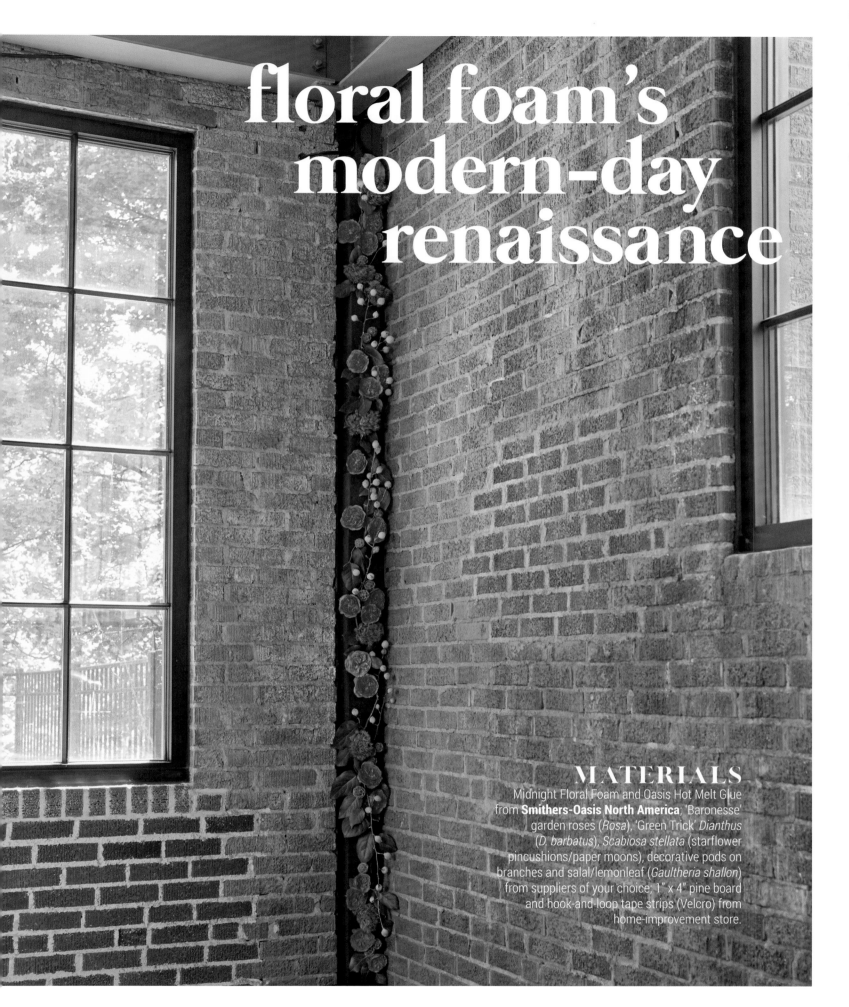

floral foam's modern-day renaissance

MATERIALS
Midnight Floral Foam and Oasis Hot Melt Glue from **Smithers-Oasis North America**; 'Baronesse' garden roses (*Rosa*), 'Green Trick' *Dianthus* (*D. barbatus*), *Scabiosa stellata* (starflower pincushions/paper moons), decorative pods on branches and salal/lemonleaf (*Gaultheria shallon*) from suppliers of your choice; 1" x 4" pine board and hook-and-loop tape strips (Velcro) from home-improvement store.

Cut two lengths of aluminum wire, one slightly shorter than the other, and glue the lengths together at each end. Wrap bullion wire over the glued ends to secure the mechanics. **01**

Curl the ends of the wire with the pliers, so the necklace can be fastened. **02**

Glue pieces of *Aspidistra* foliage to both sides of the wire form. **03**

Glue the botanicals onto the *Aspidistra* leaves. **04**

structured beauty

MATERIALS

Zinnia spp., Dahlia spp., Phalaenopsis spp. (moth orchids), *Craspedia globosa* (billy buttons), *Jasminum arabigum* (jasmine) and rose-hip branches (*Rosa* spp.); 4" Oasis Water Tubes (25), Oasis Floral Adhesive and Oasis Bind Wire (Green) from **Smithers-Oasis North America**; baling wire (or equivalent 14-gauge galvanized wire); wood boards (approximately 28" long by 4" wide); wood dowels (approximately 6" long); birdseed; drill; pruning shears.

Floral design by Leopoldo Gomez • Photos by Bogar Marin

Gather materials: Wire fixture, sisal, flat cane, rattan sticks, water tubes and fresh botanicals.

01

Weave the flat cane — and then the rattan sticks — in a basket-weave pattern in and out of the wire fixture until it is covered completely.

02

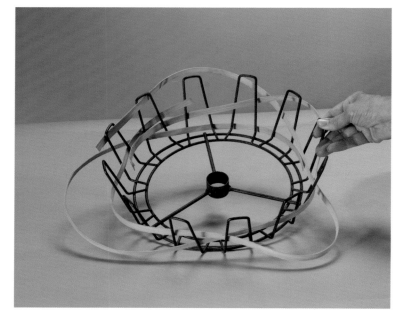

Insert water tubes among the woven cane strips, and place flowers and foliages into the tubes.

03

beyond the basket

MATERIALS

Variegated mock orange (*Pittosporum*), plumosa fern (*Asparagus*) and variegated lily grass (*Liriope*) from **FernTrust**; *Cymbidium* orchids, *Craspedia* (billy buttons) and curly willow (*Salix*) from favorite suppliers; Natural Sisal Fiber from **Harvest Import**; Oasis Flat Cane (Apple Green), Oasis Midollino Sticks (Natural) and 4" Oasis Water Tubes from **Smithers-Oasis North America**; wire fixture from thrift or antique shop.

Floral design and photos by Lori McNorton

Gather materials: flowers, plants and foliages; Oasis Table Deco containers; cork tiles; hook-and-loop adhesive strips. Glue the cork tiles into a picture frame. **01**

Pinking shears provide an interesting edging to the *Aspidistra* leaves. Arrange short-stemmed blooms through the layers of leaves to achieve the desired look. Fill in around the edge of the floral foam with reindeer moss. **02**

Affix the hook or loop adhesive strips to the bottoms of the containers and the paired adhesive strip to the cork tiles to hold each container in place. **03**

living
artwork

MATERIALS

Spray roses (*Rosa* spp.), pincushions (*Leucospermum* spp.), 'Safari Sunset' *Leucadendron*, sea holly (*Eryngium maritinum*), billy buttons (*Craspedia globosa*), *Hypericum* spp. and assorted succulents from favorite suppliers; reindeer moss from **burton + BURTON**; green and variegated cast-iron (*Aspidistra* spp.) leaves, bullbay (*Magnolia grandiflora*) leaves and variegated *Pittosporum* spp. from **FernTrust**; Oasis Table Deco containers from **Smithers-Oasis North America**; cork tiles; picture frame; hook-and-loop (Velcro) adhesive strips.

Floral design and photos by Lori McNorton

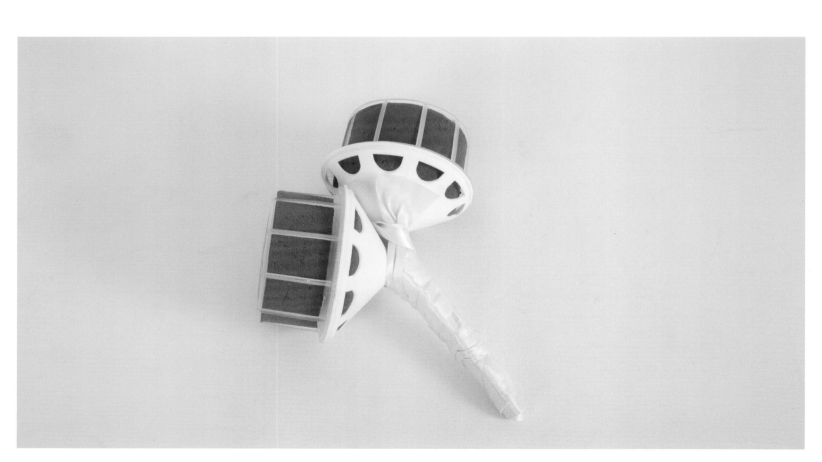

Secure the handles of the two bouquet holders together, back to back, with adhesive strips so **01** that the floral-foam surfaces are facing away from each other.

Wrap the handle with pink satin ribbon to cover the mechanics and create a beautiful base. Tie off the **02** ribbon ends. Use adhesive dashes if extra security is needed to keep the ribbon bound tightly.

lush
cascade

MATERIALS

'Grandicolor' and 'Pinita' hybrid *Protea* from **Resendiz Brothers Protea Growers**; 'Honesty' LA hybrid lily (*Lilium* spp.) and *Ornithogalum dubium* from **The Sun Valley Group**; *Dianthus* spp., prairie gentians (*Lisianthus/Eustoma grandiflorum*), snapdragons (*Antirrhinum majus*), spray stocks (*Mattiola incana*) and dusty miller (*Senecio cineraria*) from **Ball SB**; Israeli *Ruscus* (*R. hypophyllum*) from **FernTrust**; *Helleborus* spp.; jasmine vine (*Jasminum* spp.); Lomey Bouquet Holders and UGlu Adhesive Strips from **Smithers-Oasis North America**.

Floral design and photos by Lori McNorton

Floral design and photo by Lori McNorton. See how-to design and steps on Pages 148-149.

FALL

A layer of moss as an intermediary ensures a stronger bond between the flowers and the metal surface. Apply a thin layer of liquid floral adhesive to outline the design shape. Wait about 20 seconds, and then add a fine layer of moss to the glued area. Press the moss firmly, and allow an additional 20 seconds to dry. **01**

Apply another fine layer of adhesive atop the mossed area, and add a dab of floral adhesive to the cleaned snipped-flush backs of the blooms. For the *Serruria* blooms, for example, a dot of glue about the size of a pea is sufficient. Wait about 20 seconds for the adhesive to get tacky, and then press the blooms into the moss, and hold firmly for 20 to 30 seconds. **02**

Arrange the largest focal blooms in the center of the design, and arrange the remaining floral and foliage elements onto the base. Hold each element firmly — about 20 to 30 seconds — until it is locked in place. By securing these larger flowers carefully, you can then "float" lighter elements on top of the heavier ones, resulting in a design rich in depth and interest. **03**

Add the delicate details, such as dainty foliages or tendrils, securing them with floral adhesive to the flowers below. Design to the very edge, allowing elements to cascade over the sides of the cuff. Spray the corsage with water, tuck into a plastic bag and place into the cooler. Before handing off to the recipient, remove from the bag, spray the floral materials with a finishing spray, and tuck into a gift box lined with shredded paper. **04**

modern wrist corsage

MATERIALS

Serruria florida (blushing bride),
Nigella sativa (black cumin,
nutmeg flower, Roman coriander),
Xerochrysum bracteatum
(strawflowers), *Lathyrus odoratus*
(sweet peas), *Artemisia ludoviciana*
'Silver Queen' (white sage), *Rubus*
spp. (thornless raspberry foliage),
and dried and preserved sheet
moss; Oasis Floral Adhesive from
Smithers-Oasis North America;
3-inch brass cuff from **Jan's
Jewelry Supplies**.

Floral design by Susan McLeary • Photos by Amanda Dumouchelle Photography

MATERIALS

'Freedom' roses (*Rosa* spp.) from **Fresca Farms**; upright and hanging *Heliconia* spp. and Israeli *Ruscus* (*R. hypophyllum*) from **iBuyFlowers.com**; 'Safari Sunset' *Leucadendron* and *Scabiosa* spp. from **Resendiz Brothers Protea Growers**; ornamental kale (*Brassica oleraceae*) from **The Sun Valley Group**; billy buttons (*Craspedia globosa*), yarrow (*Achillea* spp.) and 'Frosted Explosion' ornamental grass (*Panicum elegans*) from suppliers of your choice; wheat (*Triticum aestivum*) from **Knud Nielsen Company**; reclaimed wood/driftwood from **Floral Supply Syndicate**; Teak Bowl from **Jamali Floral & Garden Supplies**; Oval Basket from **burton + BURTON**; Oasis Instant Floral Foam Maxlife from **Smithers-Oasis North America**; grapes and other fruits from a supermarket.

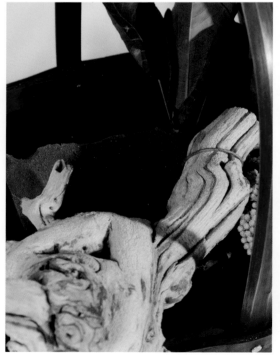

Wire one of the pieces of driftwood into the floral-foam block to secure it. **01**

Gather a bundle of wheat, wire the bundle to a wood pick and insert the pick into the floral foam. **02**

Wire the grape stem to a wood pick, and insert the pick into the floral foam to secure the cluster. **03**

autumn in the tropics

Mount a piece of insulation board to your frame of choice. Glue or tape **01** a sturdy piece of cardboard or other similar material to the back of the insulation board for additional support. Paint both the front and back white, and let dry.

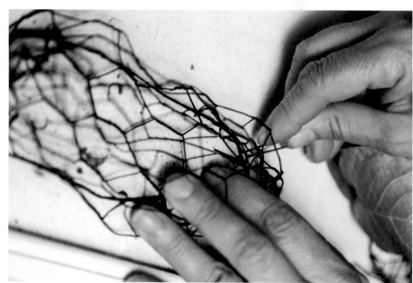

Make hairpins from 18-gauge wire. Pin several egg-shaped wads of **02** florist netting (chicken wire) or half of a plastic egg to the insulation board, along all sides of the frame's perimeter.

With the frame horizontal on a flat surface, arrange all the flowers and **03** greenery into the florist-netting wads or plastic cages. You can use floral foam, water tubes or no water source, depending on flowers' water requirements, weather/temperature and how long the piece needs to look fresh.

Place the flower-covered frame on an easel or table easel to ensure all the **04** flowers and greenery are secure, and add any final flowers and/or foliage. *TIP:* Laminate the sign you intend to place in the center of the frame to ensure it will not get wet. Secure the sign into the center of the frame, on top of the painted insulation board, with adhesive dashes.

sign of the times

MATERIALS

'Limelight' panicle Hydrangeas (*H. paniculata*), 'Quicksand' hybrid tea roses and 'Pink Majolika' and 'White Majolika' spray roses (*Rosa* spp.), bishop's weed/Queen Anne's lace (*Ammi majus*), carnations (*Dianthus caryophyllus*), olive (*Olea europaea*), *Camellia*, salal/lemon leaf (*Gaultheria shallon*) and willow (*Salix* spp.) from **DVFlora**; UGlu Adhesive Dashes, Oasis Florist Wire (18 gauge) and Oasis Florist Netting (Green) from **Smithers-Oasis North America**; (alternatively, you can use Egg plastic armatures/cages from **Holly Heider Chapple Exclusively for Syndicate Sales** in place of florist netting); Aquafoam or Aquatubes from **Syndicate Sales**; Colortool Spray (Flat White) from **Design Master Color Tool**; insulation board from hardware store; picture frame from craft store or flea market.

Floral design by Holly Heider Chapple • Photos by Alex Mangione Photography • Sponsored by **DVFLORA** *We Deliver Freshness*

Lightly spray stems of flat seeded *Eucalyptus* with gold paint. **01**

Cut 12-inch strips of your chosen ribbon, and separate small stems of *Eucalyptus*. **02**

Fold each ribbon strip in half to create a loop, and wire the ends together along with several small stems of *Eucalyptus*. Wire these loops into the top of the wreath to create a large composite bow. **03**

tailored wreath

MATERIALS

The Original Magnolia Wreath, 36-inch, from **The Magnolia Company**; natural reindeer moss from **Knud Nielsen Company**; flat seeded *Eucalyptus* from favorite supplier; Gold Lumina Modern Metals spray from **Design Master Color Tool**; ribbon from **d.stevens**; Bind Wire (Green) from **Smithers-Oasis North America**.

Floral design and photos by Lori McNorton

01 Carve a well into a foam pumpkin large enough to accommodate a plastic liner or other container. Coat the pumpkin with Crema übermatte spray. When dry, set the design tray and floral foam into the carving.

02 Secure the *Tillandsia* into the floral foam with greening pins.

03 Spray the *Banksia* foliage with Gray Flannel Colortool Spray.

MATERIALS

'Eskimo' roses from **Virgin Farms Direct**; *Hydrangeas* and white Oriental lilies from **The Sun Valley Group**; 'Million Stars' *Gypsophila* from **Danziger**; *Banksia* foliage from **Resendiz Brothers Protea Growers**; *Tillandsia xerographica* (air plant) from **Florabundance**; birch branches and carvable foam pumpkin from favorite suppliers; crow figurine from **Melrose International**; Velvet Halloween black ribbon from **Reliant Ribbons Bows & Trims**; übermatte (Crema), Colortool Spray (Gray Flannel) and Glossy Spray (Glossy Black) from **Design Master Color Tool**; 6-inch Lomey Design Dish, Oasis Floral Foam Maxlife and Oasis Greening Pins from **Smithers-Oasis North America**.

ghostly gourd

Floral design and photos by Lori McNorton

The dress is made of three key and separate sections that are sewn together to create one silhouette. You will need to purchase or make a bodice, smooth-form skirt that reaches below the knees, and three yards of ruffles to make the flare at the bottom of the dress. You will also need large pieces of white felt that will serve as overlays between the structural pieces and the botanicals. The white felt patches should be glued, one section at a time with fabric glue, prior to adding any flowers or foliage. **01**

Place all pieces onto a tailor dressmaker form or mannequin, ensuring first that they will fit you or your model well once the completed dress is ready to wear. *TIP:* If possible, work in a cold room throughout the design and construction process. **02**

Bottom of the dress assemblage: Begin by creating numerous small bunches of baby's-breath that are secured with Oasis Bind Wire and trimmed approximately 2 inches in length. Then glue, with Oasis Floral Adhesive, each small bunch to the ruffles, working from bottom to top, in horizontal rows, one row at a time. Ruffle material is necessary to work with because it shapes the flared silhouette and provides the airy feel at the bottom of the dress. Once the ruffle section is complete, mist it thoroughly with water, roll it up, place in a plastic bag and refrigerate. *TIP:* Sections of the dress can be made over several days. **03**

Glue large white felt patches to the skirt with fabric glue. When dry, glue the rose petals onto the skirt with Oasis Floral Adhesive, one petal at a time, working from bottom to top, one horizontal row at a time. Make sure to overlay the petals because they will shrink a little during the process. Use the liquid floral adhesive sparingly. Mist the petals periodically to keep them hydrated. Place the skirt back into appropriate cooled environment if you are not ready to create the bodice. **04**

Repeat same process for the bodice. With fabric glue, adhere large white felt patches to the bodice, and allow time for it to dry. When dry, glue the rose petals onto the skirt, one petal at a time, again from bottom to top, one horizontal row at a time, with Oasis Floral Adhesive. Make sure to overlay the petals because they will shrink during the process. Overall, the rows should have the symmetry and overlapping texture of fish scales. **05**

Sew and/or attach with fabric glue all three pieces together. Once dry, the dress is ready to wear. **06**

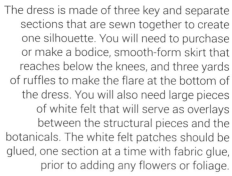

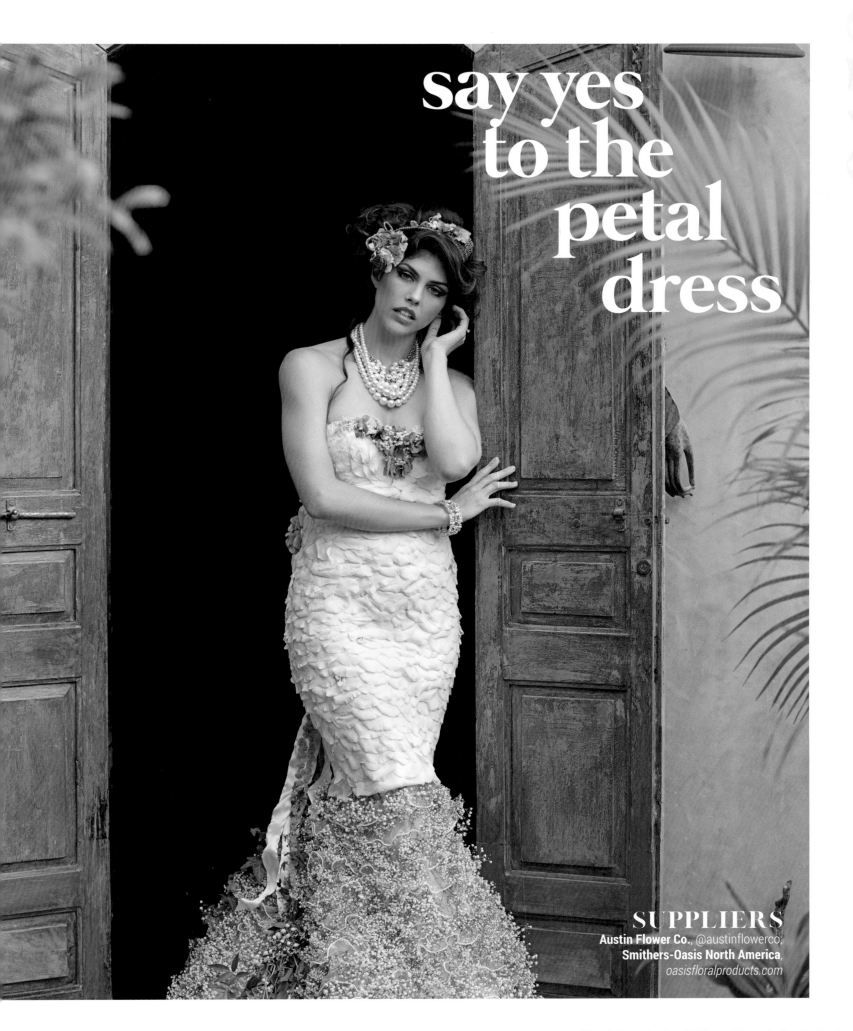

say yes to the petal dress

SUPPLIERS
Austin Flower Co., @austinflowerco;
Smithers-Oasis North America,
oasisfloralproducts.com

Floral design by Carol Jillian • Photos by Rustin Gudim

MATERIALS

Hydrangea 'Amethyst', 'Revolution' and Pink; *Zantedeschia* 'Captain Melrose'; *Kalanchoe* 'Delicate Pink'; *Lisianthus/Eustoma* Rose; *Tulipa* 'Fox Trot'; and *Lilium* roselily 'Isabella' from **The Sun Valley Group**; *Gypsophila* 'Cosmic' from **Danizger - "Dan" Flower Farm**; *Hedera helix* (English ivy) from supplier of your choice; 18" Raquettes Holder and 36" Raquettes Holder from **Smithers-Oasis North America**; Biltmore Stand from **Accent Décor**.

Prepare and hydrate two poly-film-wrapped floral-foam holders, and secure to shorter holder to the upper section of the stand and the longer holder to the lower section. **01**

Arrange *Hydrangeas* by color in irregularly shaped and sized groupings on the bottom tier. Repeat the same process using the baby's-breath. Finish the lower tier with groupings of tulips and ivy. **02**

Similarly arrange flowers for the upper tier's design in groupings, by flower, color and texture. **03**

Complete the composition by arranging callas in the top tier, in a waterfall style, to fill some of the negative space between, and visually join, the two tiers. **04**

standing ovation

Floral design and photos by Lori McNorton

Wire and tape delicate stems. **01**

Start laying individual blossoms atop a sprig of rosemary. **02**

Add a raspberry sprig, and position a wired stem of rose hips or tiny crab-apples at the base. **03**

Bind all stems with stem wrap. **04**

Camouflage the binding point with a wrapping of raffia, and tie in the back. **05**

Wire flower heads and fruits, and tape with stem wrap. Tape in bits and pieces of other botanicals. Cover the binding points with wrappings of raffia. **06**

MATERIALS

Allium spp., rosemary (*Rosmarinus* spp.); raspberry (*Rubus* spp.); rose hips (*Rosa*) or miniature crab apples (*Malus* spp.); honeysuckle (*Lonicera* spp.); raffia; Pruning shears or other wire/stem cutters; Oasis Florist Wire (24 guage) and Floratape Stem Wrap from **Smithers-Oasis Company**

tuscan boutonnières

Floral designs by Susan McLeary • Photos by Amanda Dumouchelle

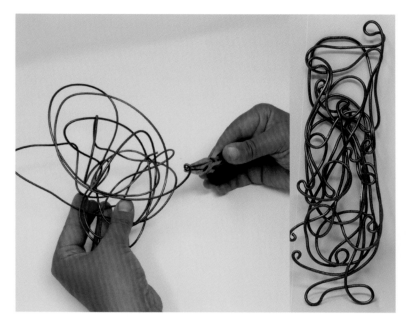

CUFF: **01**

Loosely tangle a length of metallic wire, and create random and interesting twists and swirls with needle-nose pliers. Shape into a long, narrow rectangle; the width should be the desired width of the cuff, and the rectangle should be just long enough to form around the wrist securely.

Glue miniature *Phalaenopsis* orchids onto the wire armature with liquid floral adhesive. Make sure the orchids will be on top of the wrist when the cuff is worn. Glue in the remaining botanicals. Allow the glue to set. Then form the wire cuff to the wrist. Use the glue sparingly. **02**

EARRINGS: **01**

Wad and bunch metallic and bullion wire together into a flat disc, and then create a second one as identical to the first as possible. Make sure the shape and size is appropriate with what it is being worn (e.g., collar/no collar, shirt or dress, hair up or down, etc.). Secure earring hooks to the wire discs.

With the wire discs on a horizontal surface, glue miniature *Phalaenopsis* orchids first onto the wire discs with liquid floral adhesive, and then add the other botanicals. Allow glue to set before moving or hanging the earrings. **02**

jet-set jewelry

MATERIALS

Miniature moth orchids (*Phalaenopsis* spp.), tutsan/St. John's wort (*Hypericum androsaemum*), horsetail (*Equisetum hyemale*), yarrow (*Achillea filipendulina*) and fern (*Nephrolepis* spp.) from suppliers of your choice; Oasis Metallic Wire, Oasis Bullion Wire, Oasis Etched Wire and Oasis Floral Adhesive from **Smithers-Oasis North America**; hook earring wires from craft store.

Floral design by Yoli LaGuerre, AIFD, EMC

Cut floral netting (chicken wire) to the desired length – in this case, approximately half the circumference of the chair. Lay the floral netting on a flat work surface. **01**

Place foraged foliage – we used *Quercus* (oak) – in the center of the netting, with all stems laying the same direction. **02**

Roll the foliage-centered floral netting into a "tube." Crimp the "tube" closed as you work down the length. Adjust and add foliage as needed, to create an evenly filled "tube." **03**

Secure the structure with cable ties. **04**

Attach the foliage-filled netting "tube" to the chair edge with cable ties, inserting the ties through the weave of the rattan. **05**

For maximum flower life, place blooms individually into water tubes filled with flower-food solution. **06**

Add more foliage to camouflage the floral netting, then insert flower tubes with larger, more prominent flowers into the structure. Step back, assess and continue. **07**

Continue arranging flowers and foliage, including smaller blooms, until the desired fullness and look is achieved. Mist with a finishing spray. **08**

The roses we used, from Royal Flowers, were exceptionally sturdy and did not require water tubes. Our chairs looked fresh, days later. **09**

chair embellishment

MATERIALS
Roses (*Rosa* spp.) from **Royal Flowers Group**; all other flowers and foliages from **Mayesh Wholesale Florist**; Oasis Florist Netting, Oasis Water Tubes and Floralife Crowning Glory Solution from **Smithers-Oasis North America**; cable ties from hardware store.

Floral design by Susan McLeary • Photos by Amanda Dumouchelle

MATERIALS

Hydrangea spp. and spray roses (*Rosa* spp.) from **The Sun Valley Group**; bull bay (*Magnolia grandiflora*) garland, gold Leyland cypress (*Cupressus × leylandii*) and gold nagi (*Podocarpus nagi*) from **FernTrust**; Lotus Pod (*Nelumbo* spp.) Mosscoat Stem from **Knud Nielsen Company**; Ringneck pheasant feathers, Lady Amherst pheasant feathers and Golden pheasant feathers from **Zucker Feather Products**; mountain ash berries from favorite supplier; 3" x 9" and 3" x 5" Patrician Candles Pillars from **Candle Artisans**; 4-inch Rose Petal Ribbon (Gold) from **Harvest Import**; red vase from **burton + BURTON**; Oasis Water Tubes and Oasis Bind Wire from **Smithers-Oasis North America**.

Secure stems of gold Leyland cypress and nagi into the ready-made *Magnolia* garland with paper-covered wire. Intersperse the golden greenery evenly throughout. **01**

Insert the feathers and moss-covered lotus pods into the garland's binding points. When draped across a table, the feathers help define the edges. **02**

Insert trios of short-stemmed roses into water tubes, and insert into the garland's binding points. **03**

festive
feathered
garland

Floral design and photos by Lori McNorton

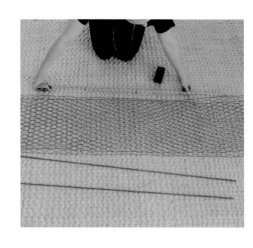

Cut a 12-foot length of florist netting (chicken wire), and fold it in half (so that is 6 feet long). **01**

At one end of the form, bring the two steel rods together, and bound them securely with duct tape. Repeat on the opposite end, moving the netting as needed to expose the ends of the rods. **05**

Starting at the folded end, weave one steel rod through the length of the netting, along one edge. **02**

Create a crescent shape by bending the form gently with a bucket or other cylindrical object. The steel rods are malleable but will maintain their shape, once formed. **06**

Place a generous amount of branch material into the "pocket" you've formed, with more in the center and less on the ends. This will help you achieve the desired crescent shape. **03**

Hang the form with fiber-covered wire, and spray it with Design Master Crema Übermatte Spray. This allows the mechanics to "disappear" so the flowers and foliages can shine. **07**

Bring the two open edges together, and weave another steel rod through the netting, along this edge. **04**

Arrange the statice, baby's-breath and white-tinted plumosa fern, into the wire/branch armature without a water source. Place the *Stephanotis* vines into water picks, and add them into the design. If any stems feel like they may slip out, simply weave them through the netting to secure. **08**

captivating crescent

MATERIALS

Stephanotis floribunda (Madagascar jasmine) and *Limonium sinuatum* (statice) from **Rosa Flora**; *Gypsophila paniculata* (baby's breath), *Asparagus setaceus* (plumosa fern) and grapevine or other flexible dried branch, such as curly willow, from suppliers of your choice; Design Master Übermatte Spray (Crema) from **Design Master Color Tool**; Oasis Rustic Wire (Brown) and 12" Oasis Florist Netting (Green) from **Smithers-Oasis North America**; 4" Single Anchor Aquapics from **Syndicate Sales**; ¼"-diameter steel rods and heavy-duty duct tape from hardware store.

Floral design by Susan McLeary • Photos by Amanda Dumouchelle • Sponsored by

DESIGN MASTER

Arthur Williams, **AIFD**, **EMC**, **CPF**, is the owner of **Babylon Floral Design** in Denver, Colo. He has a background in gardening, sculpture and photography and is widely known for his spectacular floral headpieces and other types of cutting-edge floral art. Arthur's floral designs have been featured in many magazines and books worldwide. He is a member of the **American Institute of Floral Designers** (**AIFD**), has received his **European Master Certificate** (**EMC**), and is a **Colorado Certified [Professional] Florist** (**CPF**).

Carol Jillian grew up in Kamakura, Japan and the appreciation of stark aesthetic is visible in her design. She is fascinated with botanical and floral couture, only creating pieces that inspire fluidity between the human body and botanicals, endlessly reimagining the possibilities of floral and botanical couture.

Françoise Weeks, born in Belgium, has infused her work with a quintessential European reverence for flowers and nature. Combined with creativity and mechanical ingenuity, she has crystalized her singular style of "Textural Woodlands" and "Botanical Haute Couture" pieces, garnering a global following. Françoise's studio is located in Portland, Ore. Her innovation and love of teaching brought her to the Flower School Cohim in China, the Academy of Floral Art in Exeter, England, studios in Australia and Mexico, workshops at **Mayesh Wholesale Florist** and **Florabundance** and to the La Jolla and Memphis garden clubs.

Deborah De La Flor's talent, innovative style and passion for flowers have made her a world-renowned floral designer. For more than 30 years, she has traveled the world, sharing her love for the floral industry through design presentations, seminars, competitions and commentary. She was inducted into the **American Institute of Floral Designers** (**AIFD**) in 1996 and into the **Professional Floral Communicators International** (**PFCI**) in 2006. She has owned **De La Flor Gardens** in Fort Lauderdale, Fla., for more than 30 years.

FEATURED

Frank Feysa, **AIFD**, **PFCI**, has been involved in the floral industry for more than 30 years as a retail shop owner, event designer, educator and commercial print designer. In addition to owning a specialty floral event company, he currently serves as a design director for the **Smithers-Oasis Company**. Frank is a member of the **American Institute of Floral Designers** (**AIFD**) and **Professional Floral Communicators International** (**PFCI**), and he was named Ohio Florist's Association "Designer of the Year" in 2010.

Born in Scotland, **Ian Prosser**, **AIFD**, **AAF**, **PFCI**, **NDSF**, began his floral career more than 40 years ago, eventually owning three successful florist shops in Glasgow. Today, Ian owns **Botanica International Design & Décor Studio**, a full-service event design and décor company that he started in 1989, and **Ian Prosser Productions**, his design division for über creative and high-end events, both of which are based in Tampa, Fla.

Holly Heider Chapple is the creative visionary behind **Holly Heider Chapple Flowers**. A longtime resident of Loudoun County Virginia, Holly is a highly recognized and sought-after floral designer whose work has been published in a number of prestigious publications and can regularly be found in top industry blogs. With more than 20 years of successful business experience behind her, Holly now serves as a teacher, speaker and mentor for other professionals in the wedding industry, especially within the **Chapple Designers** organization. Having raised seven children, and recognizing her most important life role as a mother, Holly appreciates also being known as "Flower Mamma" among this network of industry professionals.

Judith Blacklock is a renowned British floral designer and educator and a prolific author. Founder of **The Judith Blacklock Flower School** in London, she has been teaching for more than 30 years. She also is the author of 16 floral design books and a fellow of the U.K.'s Chartered Institute of Horticulture. Judith has provided her expertise for many high-profile floral events around the world as well as to the British Royal Family.

DESIGNERS

Katharina Stuart, **AIFD**, **CCF**, is the owner of **Katharina Stuart Floral Art & Design** in El Cerrito, Calif. She is a member of the **American Institute of Floral Designers** (**AIFD**), is a **California Certified Florist** (**CCF**) and is certified by the **Swiss Floral Association** (**SFV**). During her 25-year floral career, Katharina has won numerous national and regional floral design competitions, including the 2018 FTD America's Cup, and she represented the United States in the FTD World Cup 2019, in Philadelphia, Pa.

Leopoldo Gómez is a renowned international teacher of floral design based in Mexico City. His style is widely acclaimed and sought after for its striking color palettes, vivid combinations of textures, and masterfully crafted armatures and structures. He describes his work as "introspective" wherein the essence of nature can be perceived and intrinsic treasures can be discovered. His captivating body of work has been published in numerous periodicals including *Florists' Review* (USA), *Fleur Créatif* (Belgium), *Flowers&* (USA), *Today Magazine* (Korea), *Revista Clip* (Spain), and *Nacre* (France), and Isabel Gilbert Palmer's trendsetting book, *Formidable Florists* (2015).

Lori McNorton's career in the floral industry spans nearly 40 years. During that time, she has worked as a floral designer in various retail flower shops, operated her own floral design studio specializing in weddings and events, and served as floral design coordinator at *Florists' Review*. Lori currently owns Blooms on Boswell, a retail flower shop in Topeka, Kan. Her love and passion for flowers and floral design have guided her journey through the floral industry, and she strives to share, encourage and teach our younger generation the importance of being creative with flowers.

Stacey Carlton, **AIFD**, is a second-generation floral designer, educator and business consultant. Her extensive educational journey is supported by her lifelong training in floristry, horticulture and visual arts. Stacey is an internationally published floral artist and owner of **The Flora Culturist** in Chicago, Ill. She is a member of the **Floriology Education Team** and has an integral part in product and packaging development and innovation with Fair Trade Certified flower growers.

Susan McLeary, owner of **Passionflower**, a floral design studio specializing in floral fashion and jewelry, floral styling, weddings and events in Ann Arbor, Mich., is a floral designer, artist and instructor who creates unusual, boundary-pushing floral art including elaborate headpieces, flower crowns and her signature succulent jewelry. She has trained with some of the country's leading floral designers, including Françoise Weeks, Erin Benzakein and Holly Heider Chapple.

Svetlana (Lana) Chernyavsky, **AIFD**, is the owner of **Dream Flowers** in San Leandro, Calif., and an internationally known and award-winning floral designer. She conducts workshops for beginning and advanced floral design students, and she loves doing floral demonstrations, presenting new techniques, mechanics and know-hows. Svetlana is also a co-author of *More than Glamelia*.

Wendy Andrade, **AIFD**, **NDSF**, **FBFA**, is a British floral designer who travels the globe as an educator, sharing her love of flowers. She has received three design display awards at the **Royal Horticultural Society Chelsea Flower Show** and has been a team designer at the Philadelphia Flower Show, Pasadena Rose Parade and the Academy Awards. She the author of *Fresh Floral Jewelry* and *Floral Accessories*.

Yoli LaGuerre, **AIFD**, **EMC**, is an award-winning professionally trained floral designer. She entered the world of floral design more than 25 years ago and has contributed to the industry through floral artistry and education. Yoli has owned and operated three retail flower shops and is currently owner of **Yoli LaGuerre Floral Artistry** in Rye, N.Y. and Aspen, Colo. Yoli has been a designer for Schaffer Designs at the Philadelphia Flower Show and an instructor at the New York Botanical Gardens, and she is commissioned globally for events and shows. She is a member of the **American Institute of Floral Designers** (AIFD) and has attained **European Master Certification** (EMC).

DESIGNERS

SPONSORS

We owe a special thanks to our sponsors whose products and support brought these beautiful designs to fruition.

DESIGN MASTER
color tool, inc.
800-525-2644
dmcolor.com

Smithers-Oasis
North America
800-321-8286
oasisfloralproducts.com

Lion Ribbon
Company, Inc.
800-551-LION (5466)
lionribbon.com

DVFlora
800-676-1212
dvflora.com

Flower Farm
flowerfarm.com

flower farm
smarter sourcing

Rosa Flora Ltd.
905-774-8044
rosaflora.com

ROSA FLORA
Pride in Every Petal

burton + BURTON
800-241-2094
burtonandburton.com

Mellano & Company
888-635-5266
mellano.com

MELLANO & COMPANY